DIALECTICAL URBANISM

DIALECTICAL URBANISM

Social Struggles in the Capitalist City

ANDY MERRIFIELD

MONTHLY REVIEW PRESS

New York

Copyright © 2002 by MONTHLY REVIEW PRESS
All Rights Reserved

Library of Congress Cataloging-in-Publication Data

Merrifield, Andy.
    Dialectical urbanism: social struggles in the capitalist city / Andy Merrifield
        p. cm.
    Includes bibliographical references and index.
    ISBN 1-58367-060-2 (pbk.) ISBN 1-58367-059-9 (hardcover)
    1. Urbanization. 2. Sociology, Urban. 3. City and town life. I. Title.
HT361 .M47 2002
307.76 dc21

MONTHLY REVIEW PRESS
122 West 27th Street
New York, NY 10001

Printed in Canada

10 9 8 7 6 5 4 3 2 1

CONTENTS

TO CORINNA

1

Dialectical Urbanism and the Metropolitan Spirit

In a short and poignant essay called "My Lost City," F. Scott Fitzgerald recalls how one day, back in 1919, he spots his old pal Bunny briskly pacing along a New York sidewalk. Fitzgerald had been away awhile, living in Europe, and upon his return he found a changed city, a new New York with "all the irridescence of the beginning of the world." From the cruising taxi, Fitzgerald leans out the window and yells, "Oh, Bunny . . . *Bunny*!" Bunny, however, doesn't hear: he is too "engrossed in his private life." Soon the cab loses him, but finds him again a block down the street. Then it keeps pace, and "as I continued to watch," Fitzgerald writes, "I was impressed." He sees his friend is no longer "the shy little scholar." Now, Bunny "walked with confidence, wrapped in his thoughts and looking straight ahead. . . . it was obvious that his new background was entirely sufficient to him." It is then that Fitzgerald realizes this is his "first impression of a new thing," and this new thing was nourishing Bunny. This new thing Fitzgerald calls "the Metropolitan spirit."[1]

Bunny was now a man, an adult in an adult's world. Fitzgerald could see that, and watching his friend on the street he could see that the city, too, was an adult's world, a place where people grew up and came of age and faced the daunting hazards of modern life unflinchingly. "As our minds unwillingly matured," wrote Fitzgerald, "we began to see New

York whole and tried to save some of it for the selves we would inevitably become." Fitzgerald admired Bunny because Bunny had made the city his own, and his new metropolitan environment "was entirely sufficient to him." Bunny had become urban, with all the cockiness, detachment, and aloofness that goes with it. The city forgot about him, it let him stay awhile. Meanwhile, Bunny ruminated in public; he was engrossed in his private life, out walking the streets, communing not only with himself but—as Baudelaire said seventy years earlier—with "the crowd." This was a special sort of "universal communion." And yet, it was no longer nineteenth-century Paris: it was a hyper-new and hyper-modern twentieth-century metropolis; now, "the parties were bigger...the pace was faster... the shows were broader, the buildings were higher, the morals were looser and the liquor was cheaper."[2] Now, this all provided a forum for what Fitzgerald terms a "metropolitan urbanity."

Of course, if we tweaked the language a bit and went back a few years, we could easily be listening to Georg Simmel, the great fin-de-siècle German modernist and urbanist. Simmel knew all right what Fitzgerald meant by "the metropolitan spirit." But Simmel christened it something else: "blasé attitude." And, as he says, "every child of a large city" holds such a psychic disposition, and uses it both as a defense mechanism and as a way to enhance their personal freedom. The essence of the blasé attitude, according to Simmel, is "an indifference toward the distinctions between things. Not in the sense that they are not perceived, as in the case of mental dullness, but rather that the meaning and the value of the distinctions between things, and therewith of the things themselves, are experienced as meaningless."[3] Simmel, like Scott Fitzgerald, at once possessed, tried to chronicle this blasé outlook, this metropolitan spirit. Both men, in very different ways, tell us plenty about how big cities create and get created by particular kinds of people, by specific kinds of selfhoods and psychologies, by special interpersonal and social relationships, cultures and sensibilities, rituals and practices. It is just such characteristics that I want to loosely group together here and call "the experience of urbanism."

This book will try to delve into this experience more deeply. I want to suggest that the experience is as much a political experience as a psychological and social one. Yet here I don't mean "political" in the narrow sense of the term; rather, I mean political as it pertains to more general issues of power and conflict. The experience of urbanism, willy-nilly, incorporates "the political." Urbanism is a political experience because it's an experience bound, shaped, and defined by a profoundly dynamic and imperceptible process. Let me call this process *urbanization*.

The term urbanization has a commonsensical usage. Indeed, it is often used to describe the most visible part of this process: the demographic movement of people from the countryside to towns and cities. Used in this way, the process comes to be simplified into something that must be described and managed in purely technical terms. From this standpoint, urbanization is seen as an inevitable and natural process, and the exclusive domain of managers and experts, whose sole responsibility it is to plan for its coming and alleviate its effects. But this book argues for a more complex, many-sided, and inescapably political understanding of this process. Urbanization has been, and still is, a world-historical process, something truly epic and tragic. It has transformed, and continues to transform, whole environments, peoples, and countries everywhere. It has enabled, and still enables, tremendous individual and social advancement; it has likewise permitted new freedoms—the city air, we're told, makes you free. It has shaped spaces and streets and people and links between other spaces and streets and people. It suggests complex capital and money relations, large-scale bureaucratic, institutional, and governmental organization, technological dynamism, huge transportation infrastructures, masses of people, commercial agglomeration, diverse webs of market and business transactions. It is the clash of this particular world-historical process—how it unfolds over space and time—with the reality and experience of peoples' lives in those spaces and times, that forms the subject matter of the text to follow. Put differently, this book explores the dialectic of urbanism and urbanization.

Simmel's turf was, of course, sociology rather than literature. Thus he managed to explicate the dynamics of the process of urbanization much better than Fitzgerald ever could or ever wanted to do. Fitzgerald's sense in "My Lost City," like many literary evocations of the city, unearths psychological and individual experience, the dramas and traumas of mental life in the city. For the social scientist Simmel, mental life is embedded in its political-economic context, a context that underwrites urbanization itself. For Simmel, the metropolitan spirit is forever situated within the "seat of the money economy." (Fitzgerald had his own views on the city's money economy. He took it to heart for a while. He also took it to be a "racket," and "the toiler," he averred, "was

compelled to live in its disordered mind.") For Simmel, money "is concerned only with the exchange value which reduces all quality and individuality to a purely quantitative level." He goes on: "The interests of
each party [in the city] acquire a relentless matter-of-factness, and its
rationally calculated economic egoism need not fear any divergence
from its set path because of the imponderability of personal relationships. This is all the more the case in the money economy which domi-
nates the metropolis in which the last remnants of domestic production
and direct barter of goods have been eradicated and in which the
amount of production or direct personal order in reduced daily."

On the one hand, depersonalization and money dynamics meant
exploitation, alienation, isolation, and inauthenticity; on the other
hand, in the metropolis, Simmel notes, "one has the greater develop-
mental tendencies of social life as a whole." Narrow environments and
social orbits foster narrow-mindedness and a suffocation of the spirit, a
stifling subservience to the tyranny of the majority. Yet, through urbanization, narrowness gets blown asunder, shattered irrevocably and
there's no turning back. True, now, says Simmel, there's "atrophy of
individual culture through the hypertrophy of objective culture." True,
too, that this lies at "the root of the bitter hatred that the preachers of
the most extreme individualism, in the footsteps of Nietzsche, directed
against the metropolis." But, adds Simmel—and this is a vital but—"it is
also the explanation of why indeed these preachers are so passionately
loved in the metropolis and indeed appear to its residents as the saviors
of their unsatisfied yearnings." Thus the paradox: urbanization destroys
individuality; and yet, out of this destruction, new forms of individuality emerge, broader notions of individuality, ones with more open-mind-
edness to new ideas and cultures, especially to radical new ideas and
cultures. With urbanization, the windows are smashed and the modern
person can breathe in the open air. What unfolds in this open air is the
metropolitan experience itself, the experience of urbanism.

Simmel's ideas here in a sense complement Marx's. Marx praised
bourgeois society because it was creating highly volatile large-scale
urban populations, which although confining people in one sense,
enlarged the scope of that confinement in another. Indeed, if ever there
was a "world literature," it has to be the story of urbanization. It's perhaps in this context that Fitzgerald comes into his own. Through urbanization, he says, "the tempo of the city had changed." Urbanization and

the money economy went hand in hand, and Fitzgerald's New York exhibited a "steady golden roar and many of our friends had grown wealthy." But the tempo "in 1927 approached hysteria. . . . The city was bloated, gutted, stupid with cake and circuses, and a new expression 'Oh yeah?' summed up all the enthusiasm evoked by the announcement of the last super-skyscrapers."[4]

Fitzgerald's city was the seat of the money economy, and in 1927 this money economy was soon set to crash. Thus, in 1929, from "somewhere in North Africa," Fitzgerald "heard a dull distant crash which echoed to the farthest wastes of the desert." Later, among the urban ruins, he "discovered the crowning error of the city, its Pandora's box. . . . the city was not the endless succession of canyons that he had supposed but that it had limits."[5] And among the ruins, the ruins of his lost city, Fitzgerald spotted Bunny once again, "swinging along confidently." Only now Bunny had "gone over to Communism and frets about the wrongs of southern mill workers and western farmers whose voices, fifteen years ago, would not have penetrated his study walls." Bunny, maybe, had now seen, with sober senses, his real conditions of life and his relations with his fellow men and women; and he'd done so, as Marx prophesied, in the metropolis—in spite of, or perhaps because of, his "metropolitan spirit."

The metropolitan spirit can, and has to, thrive off this contradiction; the contradiction can fuel urban politics, urban development, a fusion and fission between people and spaces and neighborhoods. All of this presents great possibilities as well as daunting threats, for both living and understanding, for urban dwellers and urbanists alike. Those critical scholars interested in cities are presented with a special dilemma in comprehending the dialectic of urbanization and urbanism, in keeping hold of the contradiction, of keeping it alive, of showing how people—including themselves—can make it their own. Nowadays, the dialectic assumes a rather different form from that which either Marx or Simmel chronicled. Today, to a far greater extent than in their time, we have a metropolitan experience and an urbanization process that is complexly enmeshed within an economy internationalized and deregulated, within a capitalism that has surpassed even the globalized developments that Marx projected in the *Communist Manifesto*. The globalization of finance, new high-tech and informational advances, restructuring of production and consumption—of divisions of labor and divisions of

leisure—have both impacted upon and been consolidated by urbanization and urban living. Moreover, a report, produced by a British think-
tank, the Henley Center, suggests that cities are set to replace countries
as the basic units of international power in this new century and leading contenders will have to "race to win the business influence that will
bring political power. Transport and infrastructure will have a large
part in deciding who makes the grade, but cultural and historical reso-
nances are also likely to weigh heavily."[6]

That most compelling of urbanists, Jane Jacobs, made a very similar
point in her book, *Cities and the Wealth of Nations*. She argued that salient
entities of economic life are the economies of cities, and our economic
well-being rests more on the fate of cities than on nation-states: "We
can't avoid seeing," Jacobs said, "that among all the various types of
economies, cities are unique in their abilities to shape and reshape the
economies of other settlements, including those far removed from them
geographically."[7] But the pressure on cities today is much greater than
even Jacobs could have foreseen, and the politics of cities have been
skewed in retrogressive directions. As the Henley report concludes, "The
city has really got to deliver, although image is very important. They
may have pockets of social exclusion, but they will need to solve their
problems for business reasons—a high crime rate will deter investment."

Here, reading between the lines, we hear the rhetoric of "good business climate" dictates. Cities are now the nerve centers of globalization
and of globalizing capital, and equally play a crucial ideological and
political role within this system. To maintain competitive viability,
cities have to consolidate or offer some sort of place advantage to
prospective investors. Now, cities—like industries, like people everywhere—have to be much more competitive and entrepreneurial, if only
to survive. There is, apparently, no alternative. Social problems must be
tackled because this will "deter investment." Bad imagery means lost
investment; lost investment signals the death knell for a city. Image is
forever important. Cities must struggle against other cities for jobs, for
resources, for capital investment, for new technologies and innovations,
for people—for the right sort of people, as visitors and as inhabitants—
and for power and influence. A dogged, hierarchical competition
ensues. Losers pay dearly. Ditto their citizens. Some, as we'll see later,
take a stand, take to the streets, organize and protest against these new
economic determinants and philosophies.

Here, too, certain internal spaces of cities increasingly bear the brunt of competitive struggle. Sometimes these microspaces work economically for the bigger urban macrocosm and are popular because they're easily recognizable to tourists of whatever nationality. Think of London's Covent Garden, Baltimore's Harborplace, San Francisco's Fisherman's Wharf, or the ubiquity of Disney developments. All provide relatively unthreatening and "clean" environments for entertainment. And yet, in many instances, the desperate pursuit for an improved place-image has led to a *purification* of some of the more unpalatable and problematical internal spaces of cities. The principle, as well as the net result, is hardly new. Marx, after all, noted in 1867: "Improvements of towns, accompanying the increase of wealth, by the demolition of badly built quarters, the erection of palaces for banks, warehouses, etc., the widening of streets for business traffic, for the carriages of luxury, and for the introduction of tramways, etc., drive away the poor into even worse and more crowded hiding places."[8]

But the means have changed since Marx's day. Lately, for instance, urban governance and business coalitions have orchestrated purification campaigns. The methods have been startlingly similar both sides of the Atlantic: intensified police presences, so-called zero tolerance tactics, renewal and gentrification programs, highly specific cleanup schemes such as Business Improvement Districts (BIDS), all of which fall loosely under the rubric of "quality of life" initiatives. In short, they seek to transform the tone of certain areas and reorder the visible disorder of vagrancy, homelessness, panhandling, and prostitution. Not surprisingly, critics and civil libertarians have voiced objections. Is this new process of urbanization merely a process of displacement and reconquest, a reordering of spaces of luxury and a driving away, as Marx says, of the poor into even worse and more crowded hiding places? Is democratic public space being undermined? And what about the nature and experience of urbanism here? Could it be that cities burn with an infernal flame and that disorder is indeed part of the metropolitan experience? In the forthcoming chapters, I want to try to address these questions more closely. To do so, I will be traveling to the United States and to Britain and will bring together material from London, Liverpool, New York, Los Angeles, and Baltimore. But I don't just want to figure out what's happening to selected Anglo-American cities; I want to think about how we might actually do this figuring out, how we might develop urban theory and a critical methodology.

Accordingly, I hope this offering will contribute toward critical theory and method at the same time it tries to comprehend the dynamics of urbanization and urbanism. Here I seek to mobilize critical concepts—especially Marx's critical concepts—imaginatively and dialectically, not use them as sacred shibboleths. A modern Marxist politics, particularly a modern Marxist politics of the city, cannot be based on a utopian alternative. Instead, this book emphasizes the virtues of what I call a practical dystopian politics. Its central contention is that there is a dialectic, a contradiction, between urbanization and the city—between urbanization and urbanism. And yet, this dialectic cannot nor should not be resolved: it's a contradiction that needs to be harnessed somehow, not collapsed; worked through, sometimes lived with, not wiped out. Authenticity will arrive, if it arrives, by going forward through this dialectic not by having recourse to some romantic non-contradictory but nonexistent ideal.

Three prominent themes run throughout the book; these directly emerge through the collision of the process of urbanization and the experience of urbanism. First, I insist that truth claims about cities must be conceived from the bottom upward, must be located and grounded in the street, in urban public space, in everyday life. Urbanization unfolds vividly at the most local of scales, and it is paramount for any critical urbanist to know how to intimately map the city. But this insistence is tempered by the use of dialectical analysis. City streets and the local level also internalize all kinds of more general processes: urban places, in other words, are embedded in global spaces. As such, dialectical analysis also pinpoints the difficulty with respect to how local and global scales can be wed and figured out theoretically and politically.

Thus the inextricably political character of the city: my second theme of inquiry. The urban arena is a life-world in which millions of people draw sustenance and security, and, in turn, frame their politics. Needless to say, these politics aren't always progressive: the city is often the problematical arena of commonsensical misconception, a feature lying at the heart of much racism and xenophobia, seeing only absolute difference between people, simple black and white, alien and native, them and us, realities. Nevertheless, it is this problematical commonsense world where politics is not just waged but *sanctioned*.

Political struggles always happen somewhere and at some time, in specific locations, predominantly in cities, given that they are crucibles of power in our society. This is presumably why Raymond Williams, the late British Marxist, once admitted that any new theory of socialism "must now centrally involve *place*."[9] Radical politics, consequently, has to be based around somewhere and some people, and "bonded" with other somewheres and other some peoples. The more concrete question here is what sort of political organizing and localized action is required to struggle for a more socially just urbanism?

I will try to shine light on this conundrum by grounding it variously in Baltimore, Liverpool, Los Angeles, and New York, whose respective studies reveal the dramatic collision of political-economic processes with place-specific everyday life experience. Each narrative endeavors to put thicker texture to these processes and urban experiences in order better to understand both. The shift between these different cities is intended to be a shift through time as well, a plotting of urban paradigms spawned by certain political regimes. The first narrative, in Baltimore, is very much Reaganite, a mode of urbanization and an experience of urbanism shaped by free market ideologies and financial deregulation; in Liverpool, a similar Thatcherite model is delineated; in Los Angeles and New York, what's on show is an urban process reflective of the late 1990s' "New Economy." The later chapters bring us closer to the present and demonstrate how a lot of urban dwellers, like Latino janitors and single-room-occupancy (SRO) tenants, struggle to get by *because* of rising national prosperity.

My third theme relates to the metaphysical nature and experience of the city itself. This is really where I get the book's title: *Dialectical Urbanism*, which attempts to capture the ambiguity of contemporary urbanism and urbanization, in which the best and worst of human civilization—the struggle and the strife—often reside. Now, as always, but in different forms, we have joy, freedom, and hope inexorably locked in a frenetic dialectical tussle with nihilism, despair and death. Now, radicals have got Céline or Whitman as role models, and it could go either way. On the one hand, we've got Whitman, the New York loafer, the dandy, the faithful optimist, sauntering along the city streets, harking democracy, embracing the "mysteries of ordinariness," taking the city's afflictions to heart:

This is the city and I am one of the citizens,
Whatever interests the rest interests me, politics, wars,
markets, newspapers, schools, . . .
I am aware who they are (they are positively not worms or fleas),
I acknowledge the duplicates of myself, the weakest and shallowest . . .
What I do and say the same waits for them,
Every thought that flounders in me the same flounders in them.

On the other hand, we have the specter of Céline, the despicable
Parisian doctor, a darker figure, brooding with pessimism, awaiting the
apocalypse and the abyss and for whom the city was delirium, an inextricable journey to the end of the night, a death on credit.

Céline and Whitman are almost emblematic of our own urban public spaces today.[10] It is there, in the public realm, where society's scars,
nihilism and despair and death, are vividly apparent. But it is there,
too, where hope cries out: these places are the medium and arena for
hope—for political hope. This dialectic of darkness and light, of despair
and promise—the dialectic of dystopia—can be traced back to the Italian poet Dante, somebody Frederick Engels called the last great poet of
the Middle Ages and the first poet of modern times. Dante can show us
how disorder and conflict dramatizes the experience of the city; he can
equally show how this gives cities their problematical energy. That
cities burn with an infernal flame is something Dante realized long
ago, but knowing that gave him scope for hope; policy experts, urbanists, politicians, and planners forget Dante's wisdom at their peril.

Dialectical Urbanism explores how we can understand and criticize,
yet at the same time tolerate, the city on the edge, the city of dreadful
delight—the modern metropolis itself. It is the experience of the edge,
of course, that a lot of people, particularly younger people, seem to
crave. It appears to help them grow up. That cities like London and New
York and Los Angeles have an edge is what makes them so alive in the
first place. It is their edge that makes them so threatening, so menacing, and yet so alluring. Now we need to think through what sort of
urban disorder and experience should be lived with and inured—no
matter how painful and shocking—and what should be eradicated. And,
while we're at it, what sort of politics and political institutions we can
invent to make these choices. Making these choices probably requires
something more than the "quality of life" initiatives now being

employed in some public spaces in New York and London. It requires an understanding of what gives cities their frightening force and awesome grandeur; it requires some understanding of dialectical urbanism, of an urbanism of ambiguity and contradiction and conflict.

This is not to call for the abandonment of theory, nor does it give license to glorify suffering and poverty and relinquish political responsibility. Instead, it is a call for an urban theory that is not in opposition to common sense or ordinary experience, to the mundanity of the daily round, to gossip and myth and human fallibility. Critical of it, to be sure, but always absorbed in it, implicit in its practical life and in its idioms and traumas. Then, urban theory will fulfill its mission: to disappear from sight, to be chewed alive and incorporated into flesh and blood and spirit and communicated to a wider public. Only then, perhaps, might it be able to convert an ambivalent common sense into a new, practical "good sense," into a philosophy of praxis. To that end, *Dialectical Urbanism* seeks to promote an urban praxis that is incorporated in flesh and blood, that does bring real people—everyday people—to the fore, who in big and little ways somehow make a difference: they change a world that is changing them.

2

Canned Heat: Class Struggles Around the Built Environment in Baltimore

SPACES CONCEAL THEIR CONTENTS BY MEANS
OF MEANINGS, BY MEANS OF AN ABSENCE OF MEANINGS
OR BY MEANS OF AN OVERLOAD OF MEANING . . .
SPACES SOMETIMES LIE JUST AS THINGS LIE, EVEN THOUGH
THEY ARE NOT THEMSELVES THINGS.

— Henri Lefebvre, *The Production of Space*

LANDSCAPES CAN BE DECEPTIVE.
SOMETIMES A LANDSCAPE SEEMS TO BE LESS A SETTING
FOR THE LIFE OF ITS INHABITANTS THAN A CURTAIN
BEHIND WHICH THEIR STRUGGLES, ACHIEVEMENTS,
AND ACCIDENTS TAKE PLACE.

— John Berger, *A Fortunate Man*

THERE NEVER WAS A STORY

WITH A HAPPY ENDING IN BALTIMORE.

——Robert Ward, *Red Baker*

In 1991, I lived, worked, and studied in Baltimore. I would often take long walks downtown to the city's glitzy and well-publicized waterfront. I'd wander around the array of eateries, boutiques, and tourist attractions at James Rouse's pinnacle project, Harborplace. Sometimes I'd visit the aquarium at the other side of the Inner Harbor, but on the whole nothing really gripped or kept my attention for very long; nothing really challenged the mind in the Inner Harbor. Maybe that's why it had been successful. After awhile, I'd wander eastward to where the landscape was more ravaged, more uncertain, and, for me anyway, more interesting. It was obvious that big changes were in motion here, but it was a more piecemeal, more hesitant change: expensive marinas, condominiums, and townhouses here, wasteland and abandonment there. The juxtaposition of squeaky-clean housing and building sites and empty wharves and desolate parking lots was jarring. Risks, at least economic risks, especially for any would-be developer or investor, were greater in this neck of the redevelopment woods. For big risk takers, especially for successful big risk takers, rewards could be immense.

This was southeast Baltimore, after all, not downtown. Here, in Canton, while the times were a-changing, one could still glimpse a residue of blue-collar Baltimore, bygone years now, almost gone: tacky diners, neighborhood bars, formstone-clad rowhouses, derelict factories, disused canneries. I found a strange piquant charm here. It reminded me of my native town, Liverpool. It *felt* the same somehow. I was instantly attracted to it and spent many an afternoon in a neighborhood diner. One, my favorite, was called the Sip & Bite, located along Boston Street. Farther along that street, which ran parallel to the water's edge, lay a structure that particularly caught my attention. It was a vivid building, right on the apex of a busy junction. It was a beautiful, almost Art Deco gem, with a striking frontispiece announcing its business: *American Can Company.*

Activity there had clearly ceased some time ago. Things looked in a state of disrepair. Windows were broken and the built fabric looked tatty and forlorn. The place was overrun with pigeons. Yet a dignity remained. I got curious; I wondered what was happening to such a wonderful old complex. I started asking around. Soon I stumbled across a local group called SECO, Southeast Community Organization.

SECO, I quickly discovered, was an umbrella community organization, formed in the 1980s, comprising seventy neighborhood groups. SECO handled larger social, political, and environmental concerns in southeast Baltimore, and over the years had amassed an extensive databank and information archive on commercial redevelopment and gentrification. Its head since the mid-'80s, Bob Giloth, an experienced community activist with a doctorate in city planning, had a lot of material on the 9.5-acre American Can Company plant. Giloth told me that it was the bone of considerable controversy in Canton just then. The site, apparently, had latent commercial potential. The sobriquet that real estate agents used said it all: Gold Coast. Canton, or more specifically, Boston Street, was the Gold Coast, and there was booty to be had for those investors who played their cards right. However, local residents were almost unanimous in their desire to retain the main signature building of the complex; they didn't want it razed and ransacked by any developer, they didn't want it colonized and built anew for rich professionals. Meanwhile, the City of Baltimore was in on the act: it needed the new scheme badly. It needed to boost the city's crumbling tax base. A multimillion-dollar scheme like the one being proposed could help balance their growing municipal budget. But the city was also in a bit of a quandary because it had to try to appease those citizens dead against encroaching gentrification.

Before long, Giloth let me have his American Can file. In fact, there was file upon file, boxes of files, full of all sorts of reports, plans, and diagrams, minutes, and newspaper clippings. There was almost everything you could imagine about the company's past, details of the proposed redevelopment, developer profiles and accounts, financial projections and sources of funding, and more. Coming from Britain, where confidentially is the order of the day and where material like this would remain securely locked away behind closed doors, this was a revelation. Once I started to read the stuff, I was fascinated. I was sure there was a tale to tell. Giloth assured me there was a tale to tell. He'd tell it himself, of course, if only he had the time, what with all the meetings, lobbying, and practical affairs needed to keep a nonprofit community organization afloat. It was then that I realized I had a role to play: I would chronicle the tale. A lot of people might want to hear it, I thought. Maybe it would sound familiar to them.

I had the time and the inclination and I thought I could put southeast Baltimore into a larger pattern of American urbanism, into a larger pattern of global change and of cultural transformation. Besides, I knew the area's streets by now as well. I'd walked them all many times. So I would try to amalgamate two visions: the process one, the "new urbanism" unfolding over *space*; and the local, everyday story of real people, struggling to eke out an existence in a *place* that now lies "at the vortex of global and local forces."[1] Indeed, there was a tale to tell, and there certainly was a lesson to be learned for all communities everywhere. The academic in me knew that American Can internalized the dialectic between place and space. Even now—especially now—as I write these words, there's still a lesson, an urgent political lesson, to be learned about what this dialectic betokens for local democracy, for social justice, for neighborhood empowerment. What follows, accordingly, is a parable about the complex collision of forces that shape capitalist cities at the millennium.

LOCATING AMERICAN CAN

What exists in the city doesn't exist in isolation. What a building is, how much it's worth, what it's used for, its attractiveness, is usually gauged by what's near or around it. City space, in other words, is always relative. Anybody who knows anything about real estate space will tell you as much. In an old, yet still valuable little book called *Principles of City Land Values*, published in 1903, Richard Hurd says: "To believe that buildings create land values is to reverse the truth, buildings being servants of the land and of value only as they fulfill its needs."[2] Buildings are "servants" of the land, and land, Hurd tells us, is about relative location. But relative to what? Hurd lists a few things: relative to the main center of the city, relative to its axial strength, to what prices surrounding properties have been selling at; also, Hurd asks, what is the land's past history, its present stability, its future prospects, how near is it to various subcenters of attraction? Clearly, in Canton's case it was its relativity to the Inner Harbor that was crucial.

Back in the 1980s, the Inner Harbor captured the imagination of a new, sleeker, more fashionable "postindustrial" Baltimore. The Inner Harbor would supposedly spearhead growth in finance, insurance, and real estate services (FIRE), attract tourists and high-spending shoppers; it might even convince the white suburban middle classes that central city living could be fun again. The key year in this process was 1980. Not only because Rouse's Harborplace opened its doors for business, but because that year the media admitted: Baltimore is no longer a blue-collar town.[3] This was remarkable given the city's former position in the nation's industrial structure. Indeed, as the twentieth century unfolded Baltimore became a prominent central seaboard distribution center. After the First World War, it expanded rapidly as a manufacturing hub. The steelworks and rolling mills at Sparrows Point employed one of the largest industrial workforces in the country—in excess of 25,000 in its heyday. Helped along by clothing manufacture, tin can production and canning, printing, chemical manufacturing, and meat-packing, Baltimore was the East Coast's second largest industrial region behind New Jersey's "Chemical Alley."

Its waterfront fronting the Patapsco River bore all the hallmarks of this blue-collar tradition. It was always animated by sailors' lodging and eating houses, bars and lookalike rowhouses of factory and dock workers. At the turn of the century, a young H. L. Mencken expressed glee when the *Baltimore Herald* first assigned him the south Baltimore beat. The dingy waterfront, with its low-life and riotous parties, brawling seamen and stevedores, was a gold mine for the rookie reporter.[4] Fifty years later, this brawny image still prevailed. Beatnik Jack Kerouac typified it in his first novel, *The Town and the City*. Kerouac, by his own account, "made several trips . . . down to Baltimore and spent time in the Pratt Street saloons there, drinking, and talking, dancing with women, reeling drunkenly down dark streets at dawn and waking up next day in some flophouse near the waterfront."[5]

Kerouac's Baltimore was a Baltimore in the nation's premier league of industrial centers. And yet, part of the city's problem—a big problem it transpired—was its long-standing branch plant status. Baltimore had hardly any corporate headquarters. Key economic decisions affecting its blue-collar working class were thus made in distant corporate boardrooms. Inclemencies in the macroeconomic climate made the city especially vulnerable to labor cuts. Layoffs and plant closings, technological reorganization, started to bite in the early '60s, and continued unabated throughout the '70s and '80s. Intensifying overseas competition, chronic obsolescence of its port facilities—something Marx called "moral depreciation"—only added to Baltimore's economic and social woes. Things crumbled fast. Between 1950 and 1960, the city lost 225 manufacturing firms and around 18,000 jobs.[6] Next to go were people, particularly middle-class people, particularly *white* middle-class people, precipitated by the civil riots upheavals of the late '60s. Depopulation and deindustrialization placed enormous pressure on the city's tax base. The rot set in: disinvestment, abandonment and deterioration of downtown buildings and dockland fixed capital. Baltimore had 1,738 manufacturing firms in the 1950s. By 1960 it had fallen to 1,513, and to 1,100 in 1970.[7] In 1984, only 696 manufacturers remained. And between 1970 and 1985 manufacturing employment was slashed almost in half, from 97,600 to around 52,000.[8]

Large sections of Baltimore's downtown and dockland landscape immediately became junk. But soon there was awareness that these redundant industrial relics, specifically those found in the centrally located Inner Harbor, might one day be ripe for renewal. Renewal here meant transformation into "higher order" uses. Political volition played an active role: then incumbent mayor, William Donald Schaefer, became a redoubtable advocate of the Inner Harbor plan; and between 1971 and 1986 employed all sorts of legitimizing tactics and new—and contentious—development mechanisms and funding practices to launch Baltimore's celebrated "renaissance." Baltimore quickly became touted as a paragon of how a declining deindustrialized city could be revitalized. Next stop was the front cover of *Time* magazine. Soon everybody was clamoring to find out how Baltimore did it; everybody wanted a piece of its action. Thereafter waterfront renewal became de rigueur for cities, for big and small alike, even for those who had barely a trickle of water.

Yet by the mid-'80s virtually every available space in the Inner Harbor had been developed or else was targeted for development. Nearby, significant ripple effects occurred as private capital investment materialized to the east and south. Residential gentrification accelerated considerably after 1973 in Fells Point to the east, and in Federal Hill to the south. Property values in both places rose rapidly from around the $15,000 level for row houses during the 1970s to between $140,000 and

$160,000 in some instances.[9] And along with property inflation, came
a recolonized downtown, a downtown commandeered by younger
white, service sector professionals—baby-boom nouveaux riches—who,
unsurprisingly, put intense pressure on indigenous working-class populations. A survey, done back in 1986 by the Charles Street Management Corporation, suggested that as much as 70 percent of those
moving downtown to the newly gentrified neighborhoods were from
Washington or other cities.[10]

So the "frontier of profitability," as Neil Smith has described it,
edged southwards and eastward in Baltimore throughout the 1980s.
There, lived spaces became invaded by other lived spaces; lived spaces
that were invariably geared toward conceived spaces; speculative
conceived spaces, spaces reflective of dominant interests: planners,
technocrats, bourgeois urbanists, and capital. A crucial event happened in 1983 when one bold developer and local businessman, a true
pioneer, Louis Grasmick, conceived of a space called Anchorage Townhouses. Grasmick bought 3.5 acres of vacant land along Boston Street
for a measly $200,000. Forty new properties were rapidly constructed
and snapped up for investment by business acquaintances and friends
of the developer. All went for between $185,000 and $200,000.[11] With
this sizable profit, several years later that same developer built a 14-
story condominium, Anchorage Tower, a little farther along the
water's edge. In 1987 this $15 million complex was completed and
different units sold at between $125,000 and $425,000. While the
height, scale, and form of Anchorage Tower exhibited little sensitivity
to its rowhouse neighbors across the street, Grasmick's projects "woke
everybody's eyes up that the waterfront does not end at the Inner
Harbor. There is this 'Gold Coast' that offered terrific opportunities for
investment."[12]

Maybe Grasmick had listened to Donald Trump, or had read
Trump's book, *The Art of the Deal*. At any rate, Grasmick certainly knew
what Trump meant when the infamous New York shyster had said:
"First of all you don't necessarily need the best location. What you
need is the best deal. Just as you can create leverage, you can enhance a
location, through promotion and through psychology. . . . Location
also has a lot to do with fashion. You can take a mediocre location and
turn it into something better just by attracting the right people."[13]
Trump added a new dimension to Hurd's "conservative" appraisal of

city land values: the deal. Deals, Trump says, make or break locations; deals can bring people to locations; deals can start trends and new fashions. Urban spaces get conceived through deals; deals produce conceived spaces.

Deals were, still are, the driving force in American cities. And water, apparently, is the thing to be dealt. It is fashionable. And fashionable city dwellers want to be near it; those with sufficient financial clout can naturally bid high for waterside space. Thus, in Canton there's been a feverish fetishizing of water. With the implantation of Grasmick's two schemes, and with their rapid increase in market value, more and more former industrial sites along Boston Street have been snapped up by developers and transformed into residential/mixed use schemes. All evoke some pseudo-nautical flavor; all the condos had some maritime theme or label; all have marinas or yachting clubs close by. And all, importantly, are within a stone's throw of the American Can complex.

THE PLACE OF AMERICAN CAN

In *Neighborhood Politics*, Matthew Crenson says "the force of memory is probably stronger in Canton than in most other neighborhoods in Baltimore. Local reliance on recollection began almost two hundred years ago when the area received its name. According to local tradition, a successful sea captain nearing the end of his career afloat settled on a large estate near the entrance of Baltimore's harbor and named the place after the Chinese port where he had taken on some of his profitable cargoes."[14] That eighteenth century sea captain, remembered as the founding father of Canton, was wealthy merchant John O'Donnell. Today, he's commemorated by a bronze statue overlooking a small oblong park in heart of the neighborhood. Of Irish stock, O'Donnell is believed to have settled in the area around 1780. With his considerable fortune, presumably amassed from forays into China and India, he once owned some 2,000 acres around the Canton and Fells Point area.

After O'Donnell's death in 1805, his estate passed into the hands of his son, Columbus. Twenty years later, Columbus established a real estate firm called the Canton Company with several business men, including New York philanthropist Peter Cooper.[15] The partnership was instrumental in founding the Baltimore & Ohio Railroad Company in the early 1830s, and portended healthy commercial prospects for the area. Under its charter, the new corporation set out to "improve. . . . lands which shall belong to the said company, by laying out streets, etc. in the vicinity of Baltimore. . . . and erecting wharves, shops, work-shops, factories, stores, dwellings and other buildings. . . . as may be deemed necessary."[16] The construction of the Union Railroad in 1871 prompted more industrial development and further reinforced Canton's reputation as thriving industrial and port area. Sherry Olson, in her Baltimore monograph, suggests that Canton was perhaps "the nation's earliest, largest and most successful industrial park."[17] By then it was the hub for iron and steel works, oil refining activities, copper smelting plants, and, especially, for the canning industry, which began in earnest in the 1840s.

Throughout the second half of the nineteenth century southeast Baltimore canned more food than any other city in the nation. The Boston Street waterfront became aptly known as "Canner's Row." The growth of the canneries was later matched by can manufacturing. Dramatic industrial growth, too, markedly affected the neighborhood's social and cultural profile. New and established industries created thousands of unskilled jobs and attracted successive generations of European immigrants. The canning industry transformed Canton into a teeming industrial neighborhood, a densely packed place full of little redbrick rowhouses, inhabited by tight-knit Polish, German, Welsh, Greek, Italian, Lithuanian, and Ukrainian communities. Their dwellings were usually built hastily and cheaply to accommodate labor exigencies while minimizing costs of social reproduction. Many were only twelve feet wide and some older Canton residents still refer to them as the "little streets of Canton."

As the Canton population burgeoned, so too did demands for churches, schools, and meeting halls. Because new immigrants want-ed to uphold their ethnic and religious affiliations, specific schools and religious establishments got built. These religious and ethnic institutions and networks further cemented people to their respective communities, and cultural diversity produced a rich and variegated social milieu. In Canton, everybody tended to cohere around ties of kinship and religiosity, often feeling that their primary need was obtaining suitable outlets for the worship of their respective faiths. Nevertheless, they did have a distinctive shared experience, one which maybe explains their religious fervor: all were poor and exploited, all were members of an abused working class. Some, too, showed glimmers of class consciousness. Jobs were being threatened by the rise of new forms of mechanization. The "Little Joker" was a newfangled soldering machine, which, one can manufacturer boasted, "never strikes."[18] Soon its implementation prompted organized resistance from labor ranks. By the early 1880s, can workers had formed the Can Makers Mutual Protection Association (CMMPA), Local Assembly 1384 of the Knights of Labor. CMMPA attempted to resist labor-saving machines. They organized a national boycott and threatened wholesale destruction of new machinery. But can workers' opposition largely proved fruitless. Manufacturers' desire for control and cost-effectiveness meant machines were the future. At the century's end, every tin can was made by a machine.

In Canton, the biggest can producer of all was the American Can Company. In fact, it had risen to become the biggest can manufacturer in the world as the new century unfolded, and in Canton was the principal employer among all the local can producers.[19] Lots of local residents either worked in a nearby cannery or can factory, or had a relative and friend who did. It is not hard to imagine how the site became the focal point of everyday life for generations of Canton dwellers. It likewise symbolized the neighborhood's blue-collar tradition, a tradition that needed remembering, was remembered in spite of—because of?—its harshness. Canton residents take neighborhood concerns very personally, always have, still do. Ironically, this feature amplifies how a capitalist factory—what the urbanist Henri Lefebvre defines as a conceived space—is inextricably bound up with representational space, with the place of daily life. The two—lived place and conceived space—interpenetrate and superimpose themselves in contradictory and ambiguous ways. Making sense of this interconnection is difficult; living it out is fraught with danger.

THE SPACE OF AMERICAN CAN

The American Can Company was established in 1901. Then it became known as the "Big Can Trust" because it was a consolidation of over one hundred can manufacturers. It controlled about 90 percent of the American can-making business. But soon the U.S. attorney general filed suit against American Can under the Sherman Antitrust Act of 1890, requesting that the company be broken up: the company had been formed to create a monopoly and was still attempting to do so. A federal judge in Baltimore would have none of this, though. In February 1916, he duly quashed the case, claiming that "for some time before 1913 [American Can] had done nothing of which any competitor or any consumer of can complains, or anything which strikes a disinterested outsider as unfair or unethical." The judge was "reluctant to destroy so finely adjusted an industrial machine."

Meanwhile, the United States had entered the First World War and business for American Can more than doubled. Hundreds of millions of cans of rations needed sending overseas, and the company also became the leader in supplying metal containers and artillery shells. In late 1917, American Can hit $100 million in annual sales for the first time. And by the time of the Second World War, it had already diversified into papermaking and beer can production. As in the previous war, American Can made cans and shell containers for the armed forces, though now torpedoes had entered its repertoire as well. As in 1950, the company achieved a record $500 million in annual sales. War was great for business!

Throughout the postwar era, American Can began scrambling on the corporate takeover bandwagon. They acquired a handful of companies as diverse as lithographic ink producers and plastic tube manufacturers. In 1956, they set up branch plant can operations in Brazil— a harbinger of Third World cost-cutting practice that would continue unabated during the 1960s and 1970s—and its American labor force would hear all about this soon enough. Into the 1980s, things started to go awry—American Can started to feel the pinch. Hard times seemed in the offing. For example, its food packing and general can-making operations were declining. The company's 1985 annual report suggested "overcapacity and an extremely competitive environment" as culpable. This, apparently, was "contributing to reduced margins and continued loss of certain markets to competing technologies." Falling profit rates, pressures of technological reorganization, shifts in the international division of labor, lay at the heart of the problem, as it did for U.S. and European manufacturing firms more generally.

So in 1985 American Can initiated a "fundamental repositioning." Repositioning here meant rationalization strategies and entry into "new lines of business and major market segments with higher profit margins and greater growth potential." These new lines of business with greater growth potential were now becoming obvious: financial services. "Financial services," the 1985 company report says, "has been especially noteworthy. *This sector generates more than half of our operating profits*" (emphasis added). Harry Magdoff and Paul Sweezy suggest this shift in corporate emphasis from industrial to ruthless pecuniary pursuits has been truly global in nature since the mid-1970s. They say that the relative importance of "making money" and appeasing shareholders, as opposed to making money by "making goods," grew enormously during the Reagan years. For these writers, the "financial explosion" is inextricably linked to "stagflation" in the industrial sector, that is, rising inflation and economic stagnation.[20] The process is a simple one: overcapacity and flagging demand in manufacturing production manifested itself in industrial stagnation. To prop up turnover and keep the company's head above water, especially in a fratricidal competitive corporate climate, companies are obliged to borrow. And once indebted, like a drug addict, more borrowing is required to satisfy their craving, to service their debts, to generally stay afloat. The process thereafter assumes a life of its own, until it gets out of control, until the cart comes before the horse.

This global space of financial wheeling and dealing has directly and indirectly impacted upon American Can's Canton production. Around the late 1950s, the Boston Street site employed about 2,000 unskilled/semiskilled workers. For a while it was one of the company's most productive operations. Increasingly, though, the plant became burdened with technologically obsolescent fixed capital. This started to drag down profits. The Canton works had some of the company's oldest industrial facilities. Its inherited 1895 building, for instance, was one of the oldest industrial structures in Baltimore. Yet despite its evident architectural dignity, it was something of a deadweight around the company's neck. Throughout the 1970s it in part prevented the site from adequately responding to vicissitudes in the macro-economy. Space began to annihilate place. Indeed, such was the extent of impending technological reorganization and job cuts that by 1979 American Can at Canton employed just 400 people. Nevertheless, the site's death knell sounded in the mid-1980s when the company's newly appointed chief executive officer Gerald Tsai—former head of a New York securities firm—started to roll the dice with their productive assets. Pretty soon, American Can became embroiled in a complex tale of flagrant financial alchemy.

American Can would not have been so attractive and so vulnerable to the financial alchemists if the 1980s was not the "decade of the deal." Those ten heady years were immortalized by Gordon Gekko, the fictional deal maker played by Michael Douglas in Oliver Stone's film *Wall Street*. "Greed is right; greed works," was the dealer's clarion call. This set the tone. Ronald Reagan's deregulation and tax bill legislation helped it along. Before long, $1.3 trillion was shuffled around the U.S. economy through mergers and acquisitions, many facilitated by so-called leveraged buy-outs (LBOs). One of the major vehicles powering the LBO binge, however, was junk bonds. And the most prolific junk bond dealer, a real-life Gordon Gekko, was the now infamous Michael Milken. Kingpin of Drexel, Burnham and Lambert, Milken "long professed contempt for the corporate establishment, portraying many of its members as fat, poorly managed behemoths who squandered their excess capital and whose investment grade bonds . . . would move in only one direction: down."[21] By the early 1980s, Milken felt that the most undervalued asset was corporate America itself, and the biggest play was the takeover game.[22]

Now junk bonds aren't really junk at all; they're merely low-grade but high-yield, paper issued by minor league corporations who didn't qualify for top-grade investment rating. The procedure is dazzlingly easy to execute: Drexel would underwrite their bonds, low-rated as they were, for the public marketplace; Milken would create huge amounts of money—"blind pools"—raised from Drexel clients, each of whom promised to buy the bonds. This gave companies a "kind of relatively covenant-free capital that was available to these companies nowhere else. All they had to do was pay the price: a high yield to the investors, and an enormous fee to Drexel."[23] Now, predatory Davids could threaten undervalued corporate Goliaths, using other people's money, often with startling leverage ratios. Of course, American Can was one such corporate Goliath. And soon it, too, was being junked, threatened by a predatory David. Soon this predatory David itself became a corporate Goliath, almost overnight, and with other people's money. Soon this new Goliath started to eye up Canton, a flabby industrial plant, situated in an ever-rosy real estate market. Maybe it was obvious to everybody how this would end. But how was it done?

JUNKING AMERICAN CAN

In March 1985, at the annual Drexel High-Yield Bond Conference in Beverly Hills, around 1,500 faithful "junkies" had gathered to pay homage to Michael Milken and the world he had created for them. We need only bother ourselves with one notable occurrence: the meeting of Michael Milken and a guy called Nelson Peltz. Peltz, along with partner Peter May, was then an unknown head of Triangle Industries, a $50 million cable and conduit firm. Milken and Peltz got along grandly and their liaison soon launched Peltz into the big time. Indeed, a month later Peltz became yet another Milken player. Then, Triangle would usurp, for $465 million, the National Can Company, one of the largest can makers in the country, in a deal almost wholly financed by Drexel's junk bonds.

By all accounts, Peltz had long felt that National Can was an opportunity of a lifetime. Then, too, Peltz says, "I started talking about buying American Can's packaging business before we closed the National Can deal back in 1985."[24] Even for Drexel, acknowledged supporter of the corporate underdog, Peltz and May were small fry. Triangle had revenues amounting to $291 million in 1984; National Can, $1.9 billion. Notwithstanding, on April 4, 1985, Triangle reached an agreement with a "reluctant" National Can Company, acquiring the latter for $465 million, $365 million representing money raised through Drexel's underwritten junk bonds. A little while later, Drexel raised a further $200 million to pay off National Can's existing bank debt. The acquisition of National Can by Triangle became one of the first "hostile" super-leveraged buy-outs, having a staggering 11:1 debt leverage ratio. All the same, Peltz insisted he was no asset stripper. Instead, he pointed to the potent side of debt: "With leverage," he claimed, "management get tougher, they go out and make sales, and they do all the things that build America."[25]

The following year, Peltz approached Gerald Tsai, American Can's newly appointed head, with an eye to acquiring American Can Packaging Inc. (the company's worldwide packaging arm). And in November 1986, Tsai duly obliged, selling packaging activities to Peltz's National Can for $560 million.[26] Money again—surprise, surprise—raised by Michael Milken. Peltz's new purchase now bore the tag American National Can Company. Next year, the remainder of Tsai's American Can Empire merged with Commercial Credit, a Baltimorean consumer loan enterprise, heralding the "Primerica Corporation." Apparently, Tsai's American Can was experiencing severe financial difficulties. Apparently, too, Tsai was a controversial head of American Can: during his brief reign he'd sold off thirty businesses and acquired fifteen to reshape the former manufacturer into an almost purely financial concern. As one competitor opined, "Tsai put together the perfect financial company, but he had difficulties operating it."[27]

The merger, evidently, was no solution. Primerica likewise had cash flow problems. It, too, continued on the downside. Long-term debt soared to $2 billion in 1988, a mighty 58 percent of capitalization, compared with the 31 percent of 1986. Tsai tried reducing debt. He sold off subsidiary stock here, minor divisions there. But to no avail. Then, to top it all, came the October 1987 stock crash. Afterward, nobody was interested in Primerica. In the aftermath of the stock collapse, Primerica "guzzled cash." Operating income fell 40 percent.[28] So, in February 1988, Tsai cut his losses: he sold the entire common stock of Primerica to Peltz for a cool $124 million cash. Now, of course, Peltz, with a little help from Michael Milken, had reached the "stratosphere of American industry." But he hadn't done so by years of hard work, by painstakingly building a company and creating products; he'd done it, of course, by putting what little he had on the line, rolling the dice, and issuing mountains of debt.

And yet, profits for Peltz's behemoth proved equally elusive. Weighed down by a towering $2.4 billion debt, in the first half of 1988 Triangle lost $40 million. Meanwhile, debt burden had an adverse effect on Peltz's American National Can operations, which also suffered heavy losses. So much, in fact, that later in 1988 Peltz sold Triangle's American National Can division to France's state-owned aluminum giant Pechiney for $3.5 billion. The deal, in the faithful words of *Business Week,* represented a complete "180-degree turnabout." Peltz, for his troubles, pocketed a handy $834 million for a 63 percent share. Later on, he described the sale as "bittersweet," lamenting: "I didn't plan to do it, but the offer was so high it would have been completely unfair to the shareholders to turn it down."[29] Triangle bondholders were none too pleased: they had to face the music now. They accused Peltz of "finagling." Peltz, they insisted, had failed to live up to the terms of the $748 million Drexel junk bonds. *Forbes* magazine's headline got to the point, calling it "The Rape of the Bondholder."[30] On the other hand, it was a "bonanza for the shareholders," because Pechiney bought Triangle's American National Can for a staggering $56 a share, more than five times the prevailing market value.

As a coda to this entangled tale, we need to retrace our steps back to the summer of 1987. In August of that year, when American National Can was still in Triangle hands, a low-key press announcement was released. It read as follows: "American National Can Company is planning to close its feeder plant in the Canton section of Baltimore during the first quarter of 1988. . . . A number of factors converged to compel the closing of the Maryland plant. The extremely competitive marketplace that we serve demands that we maintain our low-cost producer status. . . . approximately 112 people working at the Maryland (Canton) plant, located at Boston and Hudson Streets, are affected. . . . Each employee of the Maryland plant would be met with personally, have questions and specific benefits explained."[31]

There are a couple of important things going on here that need underscoring. First of all, this disclosure, although apparently trivial, really got precipitated by the reckless application of debt; by the casual liquidation of productive capacity and labor to earn inflated fees and lucrative payoffs for deal makers and shareholders. Second, there's also a direct connection between the saga of speculative finagling at American Can and the actual asset stripping of its Canton site. Consider the following turn of events: a month prior to American National Can's press release, Triangle had already sold the Canton site to a developer for $10.5 million. So after almost one hundred years of productive activity, Canton's American Can plant closed its doors for the last time in May 1988 and fell into the possession of a Washington developer called Michael Swerdlow. Now American Can was American Can no more. Now it was American National Plaza.

But who was Michael Swerdlow anyway? According to his company booklet, Swerdlow's development enterprise was established back in 1976. Since then it has achieved "a notable professional competence in the real estate development industry." "Currently." the booklet adds, "the company directs its energy toward large-scale speculative developments." Over recent years, Swerdlow has carried out commercial development at the University Center in Washington and contributed toward an office development at Triangle Plaza in Chicago. Wait a minute, Triangle Plaza? Is that a coincidence? Of course it isn't. For Swerdlow knew Peltz; he'd already helped orchestrate Peltz's new Triangle HQ in Chicago. Now, too, he was collaborating with Peltz in Canton. Moreover, Swerdlow was applying for federal aid for his American National Plaza scheme. And in his application he needed two referees. Nelson Peltz was one, and, wait for it. . . . Michael Milken was the other.[32]

Indeed, in a revealing article in *Forbes* called "The Alchemist of Chapter 11," published back in 1982, Michael Swerdlow is described as a "bright New York real estate entrepreneur" with broad business connections. "His current association," *Forbes* says, "is with Drexel, Burnham and Lambert." Canton's fate seems firmly sealed: Swerdlow's operations there come snugly dovetailed between Michael Milken, on the one hand, and Nelson Peltz of Triangle on the other. And like his two associates, Swerdlow has a keen eye for "special situations involving undervalued assets."[33] Now, it seems, the undervalued asset lying ripe for his own brand of speculation is old American Can on the Canton Gold Coast. Now his initial "Phase One" concept for American National Plaza comprised an ambitious commercial and residential development. This would anticipate combining a 22-story condominium tower, a supermarket, cinema, various restaurants, retail units, and offices, all linked to structured underground parking. Subsequent phases included another condominium tower, more office space, and a hotel. Phase One's projected cost: $52 million. First, though, the site needed demolishing; everything had to be razed. Although the City of Baltimore supported the project—tax monies were much needed, after all—the size and density of the intended towers was unpopular: "We did feel that his towers were too high," Marion Pines admitted to me. Both the city and the local community knew there was need for the scheduled supermarket, entertainment, and service facilities. But there was great consternation, too, over the need, scale, and character of plans. Nevertheless, in September 1987 the Department of Housing and Urban Development (HUD) awarded the City of Baltimore a $8.5 million Urban Development Action Grant (UDAG), specifically for Swerdlow's American National Plaza. HUD gave UDAG money to a developer usually at a zero rate of interest. The basic idea was that federal money would leverage private capital investment in areas and for projects that may otherwise be shunned. Jimmy Carter's administration introduced UDAGs in 1978 when interest rates were extraordinarily high. Over the 1980s, Baltimore was ranked third on the national UDAG league (behind New York and Detroit). This money was used to build a fair share of hotels, some of which, like the Hyatt Hotel near the Inner Harbor, were controversial. Popular outrage was expressed over Hyatt's $11 million UDAG award when 210 of Baltimore's 277 neighborhoods had then witnessed an increase of people living below the poverty line.[34] UDAGs helped create a steady market for property developers and, like other financial instruments, quickly became the object of increasing manipulation and corruption.

Here public money effectively subsidized private capital. Money initially came out of federal coffers, but it was eventually paid back to the city by the developer without further federal involvement. Thus it represented de facto revenue for usually financially strapped municipalities. Everybody wanted a piece of the UDAG action. A lot of people jumped on the bandwagon. Few clauses set out what the money should be used for. After awhile, rather than fund low-income housing or other social infrastructure, UDAGs financed convention centers, hotels, and upper-income housing developments. In effect, they prompted yuppie ghettoization in many distressed cities. Goodies rarely trickled down. They didn't in Baltimore. Many critics viewed UDAG as the greatest hotel-building program in history.

The UDAG award for American Can amounted to $8.5 million, advanced to the developer over a twenty-year repayment term. Herein Baltimore and Michael Swerdlow alike prospered. Not only would the former eventually get the $8.5 million paid back to them, but they'd also negotiated a 15 percent cut of the developer's net annual cash flow. Needless to say, with such vested interests Baltimore was eager to play ball at Canton. Of course, Swerdlow was hardly doing badly, either. An $8.5 million interest-free loan boosted his capital turnover time no end. Outlays could be more quickly retrieved now. What's remarkable here, however, was how little Swerdlow actually had to pay from his own pocket. Alongside the $8.5 million UDAG, for instance, came a $30 million first mortgage secured from Citibank.[35] This tactic was fairly standard practice by then. Over the 1980s, almost all developers in the United States operated on the basis of "fictitious" banking capital, and speculative trading and debt burdens within the American real estate sector flourished massively in Reagan's deregulated climate. In a sense, this has given considerable fluidity to the way developers like Michael Swerdlow can conceive of and roam space looking for titles to future ground rents. This fluidity encouraged spaces that conform to the highest and best commercial uses; but this facility has also triggered periodic spates of speculation and left many urban landscapes extremely sensitive to interest rate fluctuations and supply and demand for money capital.

However, an ironic twist emerged at Canton. Because Swerdlow's scheme now involved federal assistance, it brought into effect Section 106 of the National Historic Preservation Act. This meant that certain historically sensitive sites might be protected from demolition should the preservation authorities see fit. The stipulation gave a glimmer of hope to the local community's opposition to site razing. They now fervently supported "adaptively reusing" the old company buildings, especially the 1924 "signature" building, the building that I found so fascinating. It was this monument that is particularly redolent of the neighborhood's blue-collar heritage. It announced to the world that this was Canton, home of the American canning industry, and it was proud of it. Community groups didn't want a moratorium on development, nor were they anti-development. The crux for them was what kind of development and on whose terms? This whole question was soon to become more heated.

STRUGGLING FOR AMERICAN CAN

A lot of Canton residents started to make noise: they believed their opinions on the future trajectory of the neighborhood were at best ignored or at worst treated with contempt. They feared for *their place*, they didn't want it converted into a sterilized wilderness of high-priced, high-rise condominiums and other synthetic spaces stripped bare of history. As one ex-local put it, "When you see what they're putting up where you used to live, it's like sticking a knife in your heart."[36]

Crenson, in *Neighborhood Politics,* says that many local residents' "perspectives on the neighborhood are conditioned by its distinctive history and they exhibit a continuity of custom and memory in the face of social change." The ensuing "neighborhood homogeneity and solidarity," according to Crenson, "supply a firm foundation for political organization and integration." This had been borne out in the late 1960s when community groups mobilized to prevent the extension of the Interstate 83 expressway that threatened to cut a huge swath

through Canton. The success of the local community's Southeast Council Against the Road campaign (SCAR) was integral in providing Canton
locals with a political vocabulary. Above all, it convinced them of the
need for an area-wide organization to deal with neighborhood problems. Out of this, in 1971, came SECO itself, serving broader community life in southeast Baltimore. Ironically, the community's success here
generated its own unforeseen contradictions and paradoxes. One was
that the efficacy of SCAR in preventing the expressway extension in
Canton paved the way for the later redevelopment of the area. After all,
who would have been interested in living next to an expressway? Probably not many; certainly not many *rich* people.

So by the 1980s another enemy haunted the neighborhood: gentrification. Not bulldozers, but wine bars and fancy restaurants and
revamped row houses. Nonetheless, ultimately the effects were much
the same: displacement. In October 1987, the identification of a common enemy—"parasite developers"—was greeted with the formation of
another group, a broad watchdog-type organization called the Waterfront Coalition. Along with SECO, it is now recognized as the united
voice for the southeast area. It embraces eleven local community
groups, as well as enthusiastic individual members. The Coalition
attempts to inject neighborhood concerns into the planning of the
Fells Point/Canton waterfront. One spokesman, John Cain, told me:
"We felt that people from the community should have input into
what's happening in their community. . . . [and] we felt that if we were
to have any impact we would have to make a concerted effort: we needed a name and we had to organize." The Coalition organizes twice-
monthly community meetings and forces itself onto the city "by just
being there; going to open meetings, going to planning meetings and
giving testimony."

Among the numerous things inspired by the Waterfront Coalition
has been the Harborwatch campaign, formed by a local group of progressive architects who now monitor waterfront redevelopment and compile
dossiers on active developers. Here, too, they've revealed the frequent
covert links between developers and the city's politicos.[37] Since incep-
tion, the Coalition has rallied around issues like height and density of
new Canton developments and raised awareness about public access to
the increasingly privatized waterfront. Underlying all this is the impact
on affordable housing, and, as Cain says, a concern "about the expend-

ability of the working class. We are being assaulted on all sides, and in Canton it's all economic pressure." The Coalition warns that Anchorage Tower—known in local circles as "The Thing"—merely presaged the shape of developments to come; it is a direct affront to the nearby row house communities. Hence the Coalition is a conduit for protest; it aims to discover some sort of consensus on the Boston Street waterfront.

Who does Cain mean when he speaks about "we"? Who is the Waterfront Coalition representing? Much the same can be asked of SECO. In this vein, it needs to be stressed that community groups in southeast Baltimore aren't internally homogeneous. In reality, they make up a diverse array of social forces, all of which exhibit a messy sort of class-ideology and consciousness. A lot of experience and action in Canton is more uneven and contradictory than it may first appear. And it's becoming more so with the passage of time. Thus, a notion of any nostalgic notion of Community—upper case *C* singular—is liable to be grossly misleading. Indeed, while both the Waterfront Coalition and SECO are essentially bridge-building organizations, resonant of a low to moderate-income corpus, their leadership and organizational structure is heavily dependent on its professional intelligentsia and petit bourgeois elements. Their politics are consequently ambiguous, and the ambiguity is never overcome, gravitating between anticapitalist sentiment and conservative or preservationist ideals.

More recent Canton politics have tended to incorporate better-educated, higher-income, newer arrivals to Canton—first-generation gentrifiers, really—who've been intent on closing down the neighborhood they helped open up. In their eyes, the place is getting overbuilt and they now want to kick away the ladder to prevent further redevelopment. These types typically internalize elements drawn from classes above and below them, and depending upon the grievance and ante, can lurch in either direction. But this complex amalgam of people have, in one way or another, voiced discontent about the proposed destruction of American Can. What we've witnessed here is a peculiar class bloc that formed for a specific period and was prepared to mobilize over the fate of the Canton waterfront. Now the old American Can site had become a *cause célèbre* and succeeded in activating the sensibilities of almost all Canton residents and community organizations.

In July 1987, community groups met with Michael Swerdlow and Baltimore authorities to express that opposition. Armed with placards, vociferous local residents vented anger at the developer, decried the scale of the scheme and denounced the demolition of the site. Its impending demolition, they said, was a "damaging threat to the physical fiber of industrial Canton." Accordingly, they would "vigorously lobby against this misguided trashing of our heritage." Later on, in February 1988, and with mounting controversy and publicity, Baltimore's Planning Department was forced to reject Swerdlow's tower component. This capitulation was regarded as a major victory for east side residents.[38] Nevertheless, although Swerdlow agreed to a towerless site configuration, he was still insistent about razing the plant. Here he was influenced by a report undertaken by architects RTKL Associates. This report was adamant: destruction was recommended unequivocally. RTKL said that because of awkward interior spaces, waterfront orientations, and existing fenestration patterns, adaptive reusage would be "extensive and costly." "Assuming that the practical difficulties of marketing the stores and apartments with poor orientations and aggressive sales prices and/or rents can be achieved," the report concluded, "the project still would not yield a profit or reasonable return on equity. Therefore the rehabilitation of the existing buildings is not an economically viable alternative."

The Waterfront Coalition, on the other hand, thought that the developer had paid only lip service to the possibility of adaptive reusage. After all, that threatened "economic viability." Meanwhile, responding to the Section 106 orderings, the Advisory Council for Historic Preservation (ACHP) in Washington carried out its own investigation. ACHP believed that "more careful consideration should be given to the redesign of the project to retain and reuse several historic buildings on the American Can Company site."[39] The 1924 structure, they thought, is "dramatically sited on the apex formed by Boston and Hudson Streets and its bold 'American Can Company' logo announces entrance to the Canton area." The ACHP were "unconvinced by the arguments thus far against their retention and rehabilitation." For ACHP, the RTKL assessment was "inadequate." ACHP also raised a more general point. This was about local empowerment in the waterfront planning process more generally. For instance, they endorsed a more consultative process at Canton. The Waterfront Coalition said that it had already insisted upon as much. They'd invoked the need for some sort of master plan for the area, one that did incorporate public participation. It had even drafted and presented to City Hall their grassroots "Canton & Fells Point Urban Renewal Plan." But hitherto it had fallen on deaf ears.

Yet with mounting popular pressure, and in an effort to mollify anxieties about waterfront speculation, in 1988 the Kurt Schmoke mayoral administration announced plans for a major urban design study for the city's Gold Coast. Now, at last, a "city vision" was formulated, a rapprochement between the ambitious plans of the developers and the more parochial desires of the locals.[40] The city hired the Washington-based urban design consultants Notter Finegold and Alexander to construct a series of waterfront vignettes. At the same time, the city formed its own management team headed by then chairman of the Charles Center-Inner Harbor Management Corporation and Canton resident, Walter Sondheim, to liaise with planners and the ten-member local community advisory panel.

After a lot of early hope, however, there soon came disappointment. When the city's initiative got unveiled, it received a cool response. Canton residents felt that the design vignettes pandered too much to developers. "I'm not happy with what we were presented with," John Cain said. "It doesn't seem to me that the consultant has a good grasp of what the community is like or what the city is like."[41] Many developers, conversely, thought the plans "unimaginative." Others were a bit more optimistic. The Baltimore Sun's Edward Gunts, for example, suggested that at least the process "has forced both sides. . . . to consider just who the waterfront is for and what are most fitting uses: Is the waterfront primarily for Canton and Fells Point communities? Or should it be considered a city-wide, even regional resource?"

Of course, this imbroglio over the waterfront "master plan" meant the American National Plaza scheme was now highly visible within the public realm. In almost every respect it epitomized waterfront trials and tribulations surfacing during this period. Moreover, by August 1988 ACHP's final findings were aired. Based on their on-site investigations, project reports, and meetings with local residents, ACHP maintained that "[d]emolition of the American Can Company complex will result in a significant loss to the Canton Historic District"; "the developer did not aggressively pursue reuse of the...buildings as part of his redevelopment scheme"; "restudy of the proposal should actively involve...the council, the residents of Canton Historic District and representatives of local community groups"; "the Mayor should make a final decision responsive to citizen input as to which development is to be followed."

Alas, ACHP didn't have the teeth to enforce these recommendations. Their status was more of a lobby group: they could exert influence over historic preservation, but ultimately only the city had the power to enforce any preservation order. And given its financial stake, it appeared unwilling (or unable) to make this necessary commitment for fear of scaring off the developer. Henceforth the Waterfront Coalition turned up the heat. They continued to lobby planning commission meetings; they attended all public land-use hearings and organized community meetings during the 1988–1989 period. The unresolved controversy stalled actual construction at the plant. Then, suddenly in July 1989, workmen removing asbestos at American Can reported a highly toxic polychlorinated biphenyl (PCB) spillage. Apparently, several tons of copper had been stolen from some electrical transformers and this had suspiciously released 80 gallons of chemicals. Swerdlow suspected foul play. The following month, complicating things even more, fire broke out on one of the complex stairways. Rumors claimed that kerosene-soaked rags had been ignited by vandals. The Baltimore police arson office reckoned otherwise: "There is no reason to suspect gas was poured on rags and ignited."[42] But Swerdlow was up in arms. These two instances of vandalism supposedly jeopardized the viability of the project. Steve Bunker of the Waterfront Coalition told Swerdlow to get real: "Who would benefit if the buildings burned down?" Not the local community: They'd been campaigning to save the buildings all along!

Yet these incidents were the straws that broke Swerdlow's back. In September 1989, Michael Swerdlow companies announced that it was pulling out of American National Plaza. Vandalism, they said, had threatened financial arrangements. Why, though, would a bank refuse to lend money on a vandalized property destined to be demolished anyway? This was a big blow for Baltimore. Gone now was its own financial stake. Former NPA commissioner Marion Pines simply believed that "the developer just ran out of gas. . . . he just got so tired of the whole process. . . . Maybe he just decided that there were better ways for him to spend his time and money." John Cain was more damning. He suggested that "the economy killed the project. The stupidity of the project killed the project. . . . [Swerdlow] would really be in deep shit if he had started."

This story, as I've told it here, spanned a time frame of more than two years. During that period, Baltimore's real estate market (as elsewhere in the United States) had gone into a slump. Canton's communities had played a gadfly role. They proved effective in disrupting and stalling affairs at American Can. Two years in a volatile, ebbing and flowing real estate market is a long time. Everything was rosy and prosperous when Swerdlow started out in Canton. But with the protracted struggles, delays, and inconveniences, with pesky residents, real estate in the Baltimore-Washington area meantime hiccuped. Swerdlow probably knew what lay ahead. So he cut his losses. Community opposition *and* real estate doldrums accounted for that decision.

Changes of fortune on the Gold Coast have been documented in a special *Baltimore Sun* report (October 24, 1990). "Two years ago," the article read, "they couldn't sell them fast enough. A champagne brunch on the Boston Street waterfront brought dozens of eager buyers with deposits for townhouses and condominiums that had yet to be built." In an extremely troubled real estate sector, there's "belief among many that this is not a condo town [which] has prompted developers of city waterfront homes to lower their prices, scale back their plans or hold off on construction until the market improves or they can locate finance." The inaction on many cleared Boston Street plots, the switch by some developers to townhouse developments, and the spate of condos being sold at auctions, dramatically attests to real estate recession. What's more, banks too have had their fingers burned. Many have real estate loans now "nonperforming."[43] This would have haunted Swerdlow's American National Plaza, casting doubts about his original scheme anyway.

And yet, such was by the by, because Michael Swerdlow had already fled to sunnier climes. Actually, Swerdlow's sights on Florida's Sunbelt economy were cast a year *before* his Canton pullout. Indeed, the *New York Times* ran an article called "Large Sale of Florida Real Estate" on August 4, 1988. It revealed that a certain Michael Swerdlow, Triangle Industries, and investment firm Shearson Lehman Hutton, Inc., had negotiated a joint venture to buy the assets of one of South Florida's largest developers, Hollywood, Inc. The partnership represented a further bond between Swerdlow and Peltz's Triangle. It would convert 3,300 acres near Fort Lauderdale International Airport into a two million square foot business park. The deal prompted Swerdlow to make a

major commitment to Florida's real estate industry: it is there where
he now plans to relocate his principal offices.

We can see here how those wielders of an essentially abstract financial capital have at their behest a supreme command of space. And the
runaway relocation tactics of Swerdlow underscores the dilemmas facing "place-based" community groups who try to grapple with mobile
capitalists. Mind you, local communities do have the time to engage in
protracted struggle to define place, and the nature of their "lived time"
can frequently be a relative privilege. Often it's a significant weapon in
confronting capitalists whose bottom-line principle is, "Time is
money." In certain instances, too, this might offer scope for a grassroots maneuver, as it did in Canton. Nevertheless, it's always likely to
be a defensive maneuver: a capitalist's command of space usually puts
him in the driving seat. The degree to which this is actually so, of
course, depends on the prevailing balance of power between those con-
tending social forces, and this, as we've seen, changes over time and
space, and in uneven ways. The American Can plant still stands. Swerdlow had gone. Now, local residents had to pick up the fragments of his
turbulent legacy.

A "COMMUNITY VISION"?

Local residents were tempted to view Swerdlow's exit as a victory of
sorts, albeit symbolic. Maybe it was Pyrrhic. Maybe they'd lose out on
two scores now. For Swerdlow may have left, but upon fleeing he
informed the city that he vowed to demolish the buildings and sell off
the land. Local residents and the Waterfront Coalition brushed aside
any penchant to celebrate. They redoubled their campaign to save the
complex. Now energy was directed at promoting "financially sound
alternatives for the reuse of American Can." They would now formulate
design alternatives and solicit the Neighborhood Design Center (NDC),
a nonprofit local architectural practice, to advise them. And yet, for a
while not much happened at the old can complex, and its precise status of ownership became confusing. Despite Swerdlow's threat to
demolish the buildings, the Coalition wasn't entirely sure whether he
still owned the property or not. Unperturbed, the Waterfront Coalition
and NDC conceived an alternative financially sound design scenario for
the site. Meantime, they'd convince the city of its feasibility; they'd also

try to negotiate with a developer and lure prospective tenants. This community design effort would be a first for Baltimore, and an unusually democratic procedure.

On a chilly winter's evening in November 1990, a "community vision" was unveiled. There was a packed audience that night, several hundred people from all walks of life crammed into an old church meeting hall right in the heart of Canton. Numerous hypothetical schemes got discussed. Most consisted of variations on a four-pronged theme: (1) preservation of the historic buildings; (2) a design compatible with the surrounding row houses and historic buildings, affording the maximum amount of public (community) space; (3) provision for a cinema, community center, supermarket and retail businesses to serve local demands; (4) affordable rental housing, especially within the 1924 building, to meet the needs of local senior citizens.

A lot of people that night lauded the plans. Everybody was invited to complete a questionnaire drafted by the Waterfront Coalition. On it they'd express their own views about what ingredients they favored or didn't favor for the site. The Waterfront Coalition, however, had no illusions about the task before them. For one thing, the breach between conceiving these alternatives in imagination and erecting them in reality is a big one. Especially so in a bloated real estate climate. Enticing a developer will (and did) prove tough. From a developer's point of view, adaptively reusing the old can factory would be expensive and intricate and would require a large initial outlay—that's assuming developers would get financing anyway, which in the slump might be questionable. At any rate, they'd want to be rewarded for their troubles. Any developer would have to confront the same constraints that plagued Swerdlow. If the complex was reused for fixed-rent housing it's difficult to see how any developer could make the venture profitable. Substantial federal aid would be needed. But where would this come from? Not likely from Reagan's nor Bush Senior's coffers. Equally, provision for small-scale businesses incur high risks: those catering exclusively to a Canton catchment area would be unlikely to have extensive monetary turnover. Here small businesses would be hard-pressed to pay any market rent, especially one that would give the developer an adequate return for their initial investment. Any lower or fixed rental payments, on the other hand, would adversely affect the developer's own financial expectations.

The alternative that Canton residents propounded here is roughly one that David Harvey endorses. Harvey says sympathetic urban governments can support policies of popular preservation and community reinvestment. He reckons that planners might ensure that "the transformations of neighborhood will preserve rather than destroy collective memory. . . . Far better that a deserted factory be turned into a community center where the collective memory of those who lived and worked there is preserved rather than being turned into boutiques and condos that permit the appropriation of one people's history by another."[44] Still, even such a modest goal as progressive preservation is problematical. As seen in southeast Baltimore, place-based communities struggling for any "self-valorizing" alternative must face up to the strictures of a profit-driven real estate and land market—itself responsive to broader value imperatives. These imperatives, too, condition both local and federal state interventions. It almost goes without saying that these are formidable barriers. But perhaps they're not insuperable and, in the short term at least, can be manipulated through localized struggle, organization, and robust coalition building.

As for any community reinvestment strategy, here too there are difficulties. In September 1989, for instance, southeast Baltimore communities began urging the city planning commission to endorse a community reinvestment or "linkage" policy that would impose a fee on waterfront development in Canton. This would generate money for the needs, particularly the housing needs, of local communities. Under the impetus of the SECO-backed Southeast Linkage Group, the idea was to press the city to impose an "impact fee" on all developers carrying out waterfront projects in Canton and Fells Point. The fee was a modest sounding $2.25 per square foot for any development exceeding 50,000 square feet.[45] It was estimated that around $4.5 million might be generated over five years, and this could be used to help finance moderate-to-low income housing, infrastructural renovation, and support for flagging small businesses. Bob Giloth reckoned "this impact legislation is one more option for communities to participate in the development process." Others have said pretty much the same thing. Community reinvestment, according to Dennis Keating, represents a "legitimation of the idea that local government is entitled to and should demand that private commercial developers contribute to a better planned and more equitable revitalization of our central cities."[46]

But community reinvestment proved unpopular with Baltimore city officials, receiving the endorsement of only one councillor. While the planning commission members conceded that the legislation "raises important issues about involvement," they were "determined not to do anything that might discourage important tax generating private investment." The city accordingly voted unanimously against the measure. As Assistant Director of Planning Al Barry put it, "the possible impact fees would discourage development and force builders into the suburbs."[47] Baltimore officials reasoned that impact fees force developers to invest elsewhere, where they're not penalized. Baltimore couldn't survive without vital tax revenue to fund demands for public services.[48] Of course, what's being invoked here, as elsewhere in urban America, is a "not in the general interest" argument. Thus the pursuit of growth, and its purported benefits for *everyone*, is a powerful ideological weapon, and seemingly it can easily deflect impact fee legislation, or any community reinvestment initiative. Given all this, we might well ask: Just who does city government really represent?

THE PARADOX OF COMMUNITY POWER

Events in Canton suggest that those people struggling to keep intact precious use values in their neighborhood need to face up to some sober realities. Here, in Canton, residents saw how those who control speculative financial assets possess great mobility over space and with it the wellspring of great social power, a power over geography. The Canton community offered recalcitrant opposition to this; they refused to let their tradition, their history and place, be cleared away into oblivion by the developer's bulldozer. But the paradox here is that what made Canton's population a relatively *politicized* force was one of the things that made them so resistant to change.

As Crenson has remarked, their perspectives on the neighborhood are conditioned by a distinctive history, desiring a continuity of custom and memory in the face of change. For those reasons, their actions were those that Raymond Williams calls "militant particularist." They defended themselves from rapacious developers and financiers, they called for empowerment of those hitherto disempowered; they wanted to be subjects as well as objects in the process of urban change in southeast Baltimore. Sometimes they sought to dam change, consolidate their tradition, that rich industrial heritage of the workaday southeast side. And to do so, their neighborhood politics invariably (inevitably?) had to turn inward on itself. Often, others—friend and foe alike—had to be fended off; that's why the Canton residents' struggle became *particularist*: it was militant in defending its particularity.

But while people on the Left, like myself, can admire the guts and commitment of many Canton residents, we need to face up to the darker side of things here as well. True, protagonists on the whole were "ordinary people"; they were indeed the butcher, the baker, the candlestick maker. They were, too, steelworkers and can workers, though mainly ex-steelworkers and ex-can workers, the ordinary workaday Greek, Polish, Italian, Irish and Ukrainian–Americans who helped build America, and who made America great but who America doesn't need anymore. True, too, these ordinary workaday patriots for a while became radicals and united in their struggle against property speculators; they denounced plenty, fought developers and yuppies, organized to keep the rich and the powerful out. And yet, these self-same people, these self-same radicals, were equally people who uncritically supported Operation Desert Storm at the time of the 1990–1991 Gulf War; they were the same people who urged their country to bomb the shit out of those "Arabs" and that Saddam Hussein. Desert Storm battle plans adorned the walls of many neighborhood bars in Canton in the early part of 1991. I saw a lot of them. Here's what a caption under one of them said: "If you don't support Desert Storm make sure you have your passport ready, so we can inform your next of kin"

Meanwhile, these ordinary people in Canton didn't want any parasite developer taking over; didn't, more specifically, want any *Jewish* parasite developer taking over. The inflection was legion; their anti-Semitism was explicit. Canton residents, then, were precisely those people whom Raymond Williams's fiction tries to understand. They're precisely those who hold torn and ambiguous political affiliations, who have twisted loyalties, who are bigots and racists. These people hold prejudices—maybe like you and I and everybody else—and speak in that broken language of their everyday experience. These are ordinary people, all right; these are the people who form the lifeblood of any community politics, probably everywhere. They may speak in different tongues and live somewhere else, but their loyalties and commitments, prejudices and contradictions, are probably much alike. This is a fact of urban life in the real world, and forever a political dilemma.

It isn't difficult to see how this presents another problem, one concerning the nature of change. How, for instance, are once stable communities to respond to change in the city? Cities are always in flux—that's what cities are about, that's what cities do. If they don't change, then they're not cities, but small towns or villages. Everywhere in cities places get torn down and new places go up. Suddenly new places emerge, become less insular, less stable, more cosmopolitan, more multinational, with more dynamic environments. Suddenly new bars and restaurants and shops sprout up. Suddenly these places become extroverted; they clash with older-established peoples and traditions, and old stable communities get wiped out—melt into air. New people come along, the neighborhood changes. Then a lot more people come along, more than expected, and things start to feel crowded. Then change becomes too much; some call for a halt: ENOUGH! Many who once lived there cannot live there anymore. The link with the past, their past, becomes threatened; richer people take over. Thereafter, a neighborhood once opened up is suddenly closed down again. Exclusion is prized open and gives way to inclusion. Soon, though, this inclusion becomes the platform for new forms of exclusion, structural exclusions. So it goes, on and on, seemingly inexorably.

How this change affects people—how it really affects people—is usually what sparks these people to take action in their neighborhood. Change is brought home, the personal becomes political, everyday life is impinged upon. Riding the tide of change, making it your own, rechanneling it, trying even to stop change sometimes, will necessitate both conservative and progressive political maneuvering. It cannot be otherwise; it cannot be anything other than militant particularist, particularly militant. But tensions remain, insofar as to belong to a neighborhood means necessarily to belong to a larger city. Metropolitan bigness, however, sometimes impacts upon neighborhood smallness; in a certain sense, it has to, and thank heavens it does, too! Nonetheless, it will always be painful, always tear people in different directions, force ex-steelworker parents to think about where their lawyer son, who got the hell out of the neighborhood, who made it big, and who they're proud of, might now be living himself.

RECYCLING AMERICAN CAN

The pigeons were moved out of American Can in 1997 when the property came under the control of local developers Struever Bros., Eccles and Rouse (the latter partner being the son of James). Four buildings, including the 1924 signature structure, were recycled. A new plan, Canton Court, was projected at a cost of around $22 million. According to Mark Shapiro, vice-president of Struever Bros., "The cost of renovating the buildings is higher than it would have been if we tore them all down." Shapiro planned to restore the buildings in accordance with U.S. Department of the Interior, so Struevers would be eligible to receive tax credits for historic preservation. "We probably could not do the project," Shapiro said, "without the tax credits." The plan included 75,000 square feet of retail space and 125,000 square feet of office space, including high-tech businesses, a supermarket, a book and music store, a coffee bar, restaurants, a bakery and deli, and a video store, and "basic services for the immediate neighbors and businesses that will draw people from around the region." The developers envisaged "a fun environment, in an interesting building with character."

The transformed site did open its doors, in early 1999, earning Struevers an "Honorable Mention" in the American Institute of Architects Excellence in Design for that year. The old plant had miraculously been converted into a "hip retail and high-tech office space," with an eclectic mix of "gourmet" restaurants and wine bars and boutiques. In the centerpiece 1924 building, the small book chain Bibelot had a store, paired with a "nouveau cool" coffee bar called Donna's, sharing space in the impressively restored interior, with its gaping steel pipes and factory aesthetic reminding browsers and cappuccino sippers of times past. In the fall of 1999, I visited Baltimore again after a lengthy absence, and had a browse and a cappuccino there myself. Struevers had done a nice job. The gracious building stood intact. Would there be a happy story in Baltimore after all?

In the summer of 2001, I was in Baltimore once again. I thought I'd drop in at the "Can Company" for lunch. Yet as I entered the complex I knew instantly something was amiss; I could see only darkness inside, little sign of life, no bookstore, no coffee bar, nothing except shadows and emptiness. It was as it had been a decade ago; the building had come full circle, at great cost. Bibelot had gone belly up in April 2001.

Struevers said that the other retailers had witnessed a 26 percent rise
of revenues during 1999, but Bibelot's nudged downward. "We did a
lot to try and spruce Bibelot up," admitted Struevers' president,
William Struever. "They had a relatively low rent." But their creditors,
the Bank of America, came knocking at the door, forcing large-scale
refinancing and store downsizing. Bibelot purportedly had between
$10–$15 million in assets and $15–$18 million in debts. Soon Donna's
started to feel the pinch, too, and had to quit the space in turn; without a bookstore, how could a bookstore's café survive? Meanwhile,
nearby Rite-Aid was in trouble because of its own expansion policies,
overstretching itself across America, buying up too many other phar-
macies, piling up losses of over $600 million for 1998 and 1999. In
1991, when I first encountered American Can, I thought then it was
some sort of metaphor for Reaganite urbanization; ten years on, I am
hoping it may be that era's epitaph.

3

Them and Us:
Rebuilding the Ruins
in Liverpool

THE MODERN CITY IS THE LOCUS CLASSICUS
OF INCOMPATIBLE REALITIES.

—— Salman Rushdie, *Satanic Verses*

IN A LIVERPOOL ME SEE A COLORFUL PEOPLE |
FORGET ABOUT DE BEATLES | TREAT EVERYONE AS EQUAL |
I WAS OBSERVING A PEOPLE WHO CAN WIN |
THEY'RE MADE OF BONE AND BLOOD | AND SKIN.

—— Benjamin Zephaniah, *Liverpool*

BUT IF THE EXPERIENCE IS ABOUT BEING
HUMAN AND MOVES ME THEN YOU'VE MADE IT MY
EXPERIENCE. . . . YOU CAN DENY UNIVERSALITY. . . .
BUT YOU CAN'T ABOLISH IT.

—— Bernard Malamud, *The Tenants*

Urban politics can create a false commonality of place, but also false forms of division. In Baltimore, we witnessed local people banding together in response to external pressure; in Liverpool—in Toxteth, the specific area of Liverpool examined here—external pressure has invariably forced locals apart, compelled them to disagree. In one sense, this was something of a democratic virtue; in another, it merely entrenched the difficulties and accentuated the external pressures. Some aspects of Toxteth reveal the marvels of multiculturalism and affirm diverse urban living and activism. Others highlight its potential pitfalls and emphasize that unless expressions of difference between people possess commonality, speak some lingua franca, solidarity can be threatened by exclusivity. Exclusivity, in turn, can engender separatism and isolation, and end up perpetuating the unjust status quo that multicultural activism sought to counteract in the first place.

Liverpool has consistently been one of Europe's most impoverished urban areas in the postwar era. During the late 1960s and early 1970s, it suffered massive capital flight and disinvestment, shedding jobs as well as people—from a peak of 867,000 in 1937, the city's population has progressively whittled down to 538,809 in 1981 and 452,450 in 1991 (2001 projections indicate this might break at an even 400,000). By the 1980s, such economic and social trauma prompted local demoralization over the failure of successive Conservative government programs to tackle poverty and unemployment. It has likewise sparked political infighting and ideological shenanigans at the municipal level.[1] As the dust settled in the 1990s, Liverpudlians in Toxteth sought to pick up the pieces and reassemble the puzzle. How can a neighborhood of poor people, with no political or economic leverage or trust in local or national government, rebuild their neighborhood and reaffirm their allegiances to place?

Toxteth hit the headlines in 1981 when it erupted into a zone of insurgency. The actual spark that lit the fuse was the heavy-handed police treatment of a twenty-year black youth, Leroy Alphonse Cooper, on a balmy July 3 evening. A fracas between onlookers and police suddenly escalated from a minor scuffle to violent pitched battles, as angry young black and white men lobbed Molotov cocktails and paving stones at the cops. But this was really an "intifada" against seething economic hardship and years of racism and police harassment and brutality. Momentarily, the "voice of the voiceless" was heard, and quickly quelled by the unprecedented police use of CS gas on the British mainland.[2] The "mini-riots" of 1985 and 1990 further emphasized the volatility of a city life forged out of racism and of a local economy shoved, poked, and cajoled by the invisible hand.

Since the riots of 1981, assorted Conservative politicians have parachuted into war-torn Toxteth like excited Victorian missionaries, journeying into the heart of darkness and bemoaning "the horror, the horror." They caused quite a stir when they arrived, but usually made little difference by the time they left. Meantime only their careers seemed to have flourished. The most infamous missionary was Michael Heseltine, then-minister of the environment, who in the aftermath of the 1981 Toxteth "riots" was christened "Minister for Merseyside." However, despite his frequent bus-top peregrinations with eager philanthropic investors, Toxteth residents soon discovered that "all we got from Mr. Heseltine was trees in Princes Avenue, and even they were planted by contractors from outside."[3]

The 1984 International Garden Festival and Tory-inspired Merseyside Development Corporation's (MDC) flagship, the Albert Dock maritime shopping complex, had little economic impact or cultural relevance for nearby Toxteth residents. If anything, the MDC actually drained money away from Toxteth. Whereas MDC's central government cash contribution increased from £10 million in 1981–1982 to about £35 million in 1987, the city council's housing capital allocation over the same period declined from £40 million to £27.5 million.[4] Bizarrely, MDC also squandered more than £1 million in 1992 on a Tall Ships Regatta and concert on the River Mersey to celebrate the 500th anniversary of Columbus's voyage to America.

Toxteth—which forms part of the larger zip code district of "South Central" Liverpool 8—succeeds in accentuating the city's traumas and dramas, and has been a battleground for a whole gamut of urban ills. Inner-city poverty is palpable there, as various studies evince. A 1991 Liverpool city council report on "quality of life," for instance, showed that 40 percent of the city's population live in poverty and 15 percent live in "intense" poverty. In the city's four inner-city wards, Toxteth included, six out of ten households lived in poverty and three out of ten were intensely deprived. Police riot vans, dispatched from a ring of five nearby police stations, continue to assume an ominous presence in

Toxteth, even getting stepped up in May–June 1995 after a spate of gang violence. Toxteth "businessman" David Ungi was gunned down and stashes of Uzi submachine guns were discovered locally; reprisals sparked street disturbances, with cars getting set ablaze. Tumult has often been suppressed by an armed riot police contingent.

Peeking out in between the dereliction are rows of rehabilitated Georgian terraces—many owned and managed by local nonprofit housing associations—which give some of Toxteth's streets a piquant shabby grandeur. In these streets, hatred, squalor, and violence cohabit with dynamic grassroots organizing, hope, and creativity: arts groups, African dance troupes, black theater, music, photography, poetry (such as "duboetry"), a book shop, and the Charles Wootton educational center. Much of this creativity remains uncommodified and consequently faces perennial budgeting crises. Local poetry and photography came together to affirm ethnic identity in Toxteth in an engaging anthology, published in 1990, called *Undercurrents*. Its foreword describes the collection as "the product of many creative individuals living in, and slightly beyond, the boundaries of the graffiti and red, gold and green street-signs of Liverpool's inner-city, who are anxious to stir up movement and change through their work." The collection expresses "both the positive and negative aspects of inner-city living; the hopes, fears, anger, opinions, humor, knowledge, love, compassion of several armful of committed individuals born, or now living in Liverpool." [5]

Toxteth's black community is really plural: its members are distinctively polyglot and internally heterogeneous. Aside from vernacular English, at least six other languages are spoken: Arabic, Bengali, Chinese, Hindi, Somali, and Urdu. And this linguistic diversity is crosscut by differing religious creeds. All Liverpool city council communiqués to Toxteth residents come translated in six languages. Notwithstanding, confusion, isolation, and alienation abound, especially for newly arrived immigrants—like Somalis, who've come into conflict with indigenous blacks over access to welfare resources. Here, communication breakdown and poverty, plus frustration and the sheer anxiety of living in the inner city, has equated to intolerance and victimization within black groups.

The Gifford Report published in 1989, the postmortem on Toxteth's longstanding malaise, laid bare the city's grisly legacy of racism. The Inquiry team, and ensuing report, revealed that Liverpool's black

populations are denied access to jobs, experience different forms of institutional discrimination, and are exposed to taunts, threats, and violence
if they venture outside of specific sectors of the city. Liverpool blacks are
thereby dramatically circumscribed geographically. Those who have
dared to veer toward outlying districts quickly return to Liverpool 8 (or to
adjacent Liverpool 17). Many speak of "Walton, Alabama," after a north-
ern neighborhood where Liverpool's own Jim Crow laws prevail. In this
sense, Toxteth is a relatively safe haven. Gifford also indicted Merseyside
police for its insensitive law enforcement practices in area, and the Mili-
tant-controlled city council for its color-blind stance.

Militant, a Trotskyist faction of the national Labour Party, came to
dominate the Liverpool city council after their electoral victory in May
1983. They imposed their own brand of municipal socialism and came
into direct conflict with Thatcher's Conservative government over
"rate-capping" constraints on Liverpool's collective consumption
budget. Militant's specialty was setting a "deficit budget" while vow-
ing to cut neither jobs nor services, and refusing to slash spending or
raise council rates and rents to compensate for the shortfall. In effect,
it brazenly tried to force the Tory government to cough up more
money for a hard-up city.

At first, this confrontational model worked. For a couple of years,
via strikes and street demonstrations (many coinciding with support
for the 1984–1985 national miners' strike), Militant got away with
"stinging" extra money out of the Thatcher government. Emboldened
by these successes, they pressed ahead with their costly, and suicidal,
Urban Regeneration Strategy (URS)—a citywide house-building program. But by 1985 its deficit rate-setting budget meant there was no
money to pay city employees' wages. To "solve" this imminent crisis,
Militant councilors issued redundancy notices to all its 30,000 council
workforce, saying they'd lose their jobs in December 1985 but would be
reinstated some time before April 1986, when the new financial year
began. "Happy Christmas—Get Your Cards," ran the Liverpool Echo's
scathing headline (September 6, 1985).

Unsurprisingly, this antic split the unions. Support began to crum-
ble and central government tightened its grip on the city. Neil Kin-
nock's national Labour Party also denounced Liverpool's Labour
Militants at the 1985 party conference in Bournemouth. Bizarrely, Militant went cap in hand to the Gnomes of Zurich for a bailout, which

they duly got; the following year, they did likewise, to a Japanese bank this time. Earlier highs, like its admirable public housing strategy, fast receded from sight. Erstwhile supporters felt betrayed; other allies were left cold by Militant's behavior, not just the unions, but also the voluntary sector and, especially, Liverpool's black communities. Furor here broke out in 1984 over the appointment of Sam Bond as the council's race relations officer. Liverpool's Black Caucus claimed that Bond, while black himself, was a Militant hack with an "ideological hostility" toward affirmative action policies. The Caucus said "the continual use of all classical features of Stalinist policies. . . . stand out in analyzing the approach adopted by Militant to the Black community in Liverpool," and that "the harm done to race relations in Liverpool and to the reputation of the Labour Party amongst the local black community will take years to repair."[6]

RUINS, RENEWAL, AND SOCIAL JUSTICE IN GRANBY

Within Toxteth, the bulk of black residents live in three census wards: Abercromby, Arundel and Granby, with Granby having as large a black and minority population as the other two combined. The tribulations of Liverpool 8 consequently reach fever pitch in Granby. Over the past two decades, the neighborhood has become synonymous with drugs and crime and with high-speed stolen car chases, apparently thieved from elsewhere in the city. This has created immense nuisance for local residents and the kind of disorder that doesn't exactly enrich Granby's lively cultural milieu: intolerable noise (cars screeching in the early hours), danger (some have been set alight), and dreadful heartache (several young kids have been killed by speeding vehicles). Unsurprisingly, tensions between residents and police have ensued, as the former demand tough action against the culprits.

In a bid to ameliorate these disturbances, Granby Street was opened up in 1993 at the junction with Princes Avenue. Until then, the street had been blocked off, and the social isolation seemed to be perpetuated by its physical isolation and fortresslike quality. Any keen urbanist will instantly recognize this initiative: it is one Jane Jacobs advocated years ago in her pathbreaking *Death and Life of the Great American Cities* (1961). Opening up Granby Street endeavored to waft vitality into a bleak empty street. From a deserted and threatening enclosed space, it strove to re-create what Jacobs called the "scene of an intricate street ballet," where people stroll, linger, talk, and shop, and where the street is busy with pedestrians around the clock. "A well-used street," according to Jacobs, "is apt to be a safe street."[7] It's safe—or at least safer—because it's busy, and its users can effectively engage in a voluntary and casual form of "self-policing."

In Granby the tactic helped for a while. But more stubborn problems persisted. For one thing, unemployment in the ward was massive. While notoriously difficult to assess the precise number of jobless—official census figures in 1991 suggest 41.6 percent of Granby were "economically inactive"—it's thought that unemployment for black teenagers was at 80 to 90 percent. Predictably, some withdrew into their communities and reverted to "informal" practices, counteracting alienation, despair, and disillusionment their own way. Opting out of "the system" of welfare registering and collecting of social security benefits was often a rational alternative survival mechanism: from an unemployment statistic subjected to humiliating institutional scrutiny, you were now able to tap the burgeoning informal sector. The drug economy was a further temptation for alternative urban entrepreneurship and market expansion. An unfortunate casualty of this option was well-known community worker and local media spokesperson Michael Showers, employed as an immigration advice worker with Merseyside Immigration Advice Unit, and convicted and imprisoned in 1991 for his involvement in the importation of heroin. This area of vulnerability and desperation has become something of a proving ground for sales and trafficking of heroin and crack—one of Britain's first crack factories, in fact, was discovered at Kelvin Grove, Toxteth, in 1987.[8]

The escalating problems of crack were met with novel grassroots responses. One Granby barber, Ken Drysdale, established a drug awareness project in a back room of his barber's shop. Out of sheer frustration over the city's ineffectual drug services, Drysdale decided to act himself. His project tried to reduce drug-related problems and enhance local understanding of them. Members of the community were shown how to live a drug-free life and encouraged to abstain from drugs or move away from hard drug-use patterns. Drysdale asked: "What kind of world is it when it takes me, a barber, to start something like this?"[9]

The lurid drug scene in Granby gave police a pretext for employing paramilitary style community policing. The black-run Liverpool 8 Law Center blamed "conflictual stances between police and local communities squarely on the tactics of Merseyside Police."[10] These denunciations fanned the flames of conspiracy theories, whether fanciful or not. Many locals claimed that police allowed stolen cars into Granby Street as an excuse to move in. With numerous drugs-related raids, and the continued assertion that all stolen cars joy-riding along Granby Street were driven by local youth, the police adopted ever more sophisticated modes of surveillance and repression—reaching Orwellian proportions with ubiquitous "chopper" squad patrols. This £1 million helicopter was armed with a powerful searchlight and highly sensitive night vision equipment, and with low-flying maneuvers could pinpoint suspects from the air. The helicopter was controversial, needless to say, and was the target of a petrol bomb attack by a gang of masked raiders at Liverpool Airport.[11]

These circumstances provided the backdrop for a broad sweeping redevelopment plan proposed for the Granby Triangle, a space of acute social and physical deprivation. During the summer of 1994, Liverpool city council assumed responsibility for regeneration of Granby Triangle, thinking up a sort of area Marshall Plan. Over that summer, consultation exercises between the council and relevant housing associations (like Liverpool Housing Trust, Cooperative Development Services, and Merseyside Improved Houses) took place. To broaden the consultative process, the council set up liaison exercises with local residents, inviting them to exhibitions and asking them to complete questionnaires with respect to their views about the way forward. Primarily, the program aimed either to rehabilitate or renew the Triangle's crumbling and abandoned housing stock.

But its implications went beyond the mere physical fabric of the area. Any scheme would clearly impact the future social and cultural texture of Granby, and would affect, directly or indirectly, numerous community and resident associations, schools, small businesses, and shops. Local retailing along Granby has always generated modest turnover given its limited market catchment and poor clientele. Those businesses resilient enough to survive so far have struggled even more since the closure of Granby Street's post office in early 1994 because of successive heists.

A "Granby Housing Condition Survey," undertaken by the city council in 1992, found that 25 percent of properties in the ward were
vacant; a further 5 percent were derelict and boarded up, and another
50 percent were in disrepair and "unfit" or "seriously unfit" for human
habitation. In response to chronic poverty and decay, that same year
the city council received £9.4 million to implement a program of
rebuilding. This funding comprised £0.4 million from the council's
own capital program with the remainder representing a central
government subsidy as part of the "Merseyside Special Allocation"
(MSA). This money, to be sure, was infuriatingly trivial when one considers the extent of Granby's devastation. And it paled alongside the
vast central government handouts guzzled by the MDC to sponsor an
enclave of glitzy apartments and stores at the Albert Dock.

Following a public inquiry in June 1997, a Compulsory Purchase
Order (CPO) for all units along and around Granby Street was granted
the following October. All non-housing association housing was
snapped up at an average cost of £17,000. The deal was hardly ideal for
local owner-occupiers, since the money was insufficient to buy a similar-
sized home elsewhere in Liverpool. But assistance was promised to rebuy
properties from housing associations and the city council. Everybody
displaced from the old stock would be rehoused in the area, if they so
desired. Potentially, up to five hundred dwelling units were to be cleared
away and rebuilt, though shops were excluded from the CPO and local
merchants were required to enter into negotiation with the council for
the purchase of their stores. After several years of deadlock, a lot of
residents were just relieved that any action was finally happening.

Blame for delay had been apportioned to various agents and antagonists, from housing associations and local authorities to greedy
owner-occupiers and interfering white politicians. Liverpool city council reckoned that gridlock initially stemmed from the "absence of an
agreed strategy for the area" *(Report of Joint Meeting of Policy and Resources
and Housing Committee,* November 1994). The council and local housing
associations were keen to get things moving in Granby from the out-
set, but consent over how to proceed was necessary. The more so
because the report states explicitly: "If no clear program is put in
place for the whole area this resource will be lost." And, it is "felt that
the loss of MSA funding would be disastrous for the area without
which any solution would be impossible. . . . the grant aid and private

borrowing necessary to meet development costs will only be available for a scheme which brings about comprehensive regeneration of the area." The report concluded, "The options are clear: do nothing or find a *commonsense compromise* that allows a meaningful regeneration plan to go ahead" (emphasis added).

Although the preparation for this rebuilding program dated back to November 1994, by December 2001 nothing had been rebuilt. The entire Granby neighborhood resembled the South Bronx in its darkest days of the late 1970s. Ruins were everywhere. Street upon street was boarded up and derelict, uninhabited and uninhabitable. Not even a cat could be glimpsed the chilly gray day I ventured out there. What were once eerie streets were now even eerier, even more desolate and abandoned, as they awaited extensive demolition.

"WE'RE DOING THIS FOR THE BLACK COMMUNITY"

Back in 1994, Labour city council initially appealed for a "commonsense compromise" to make possible meaningful regeneration. Such a compromise probably required what John Rawls in *Political Liberalism* called a "reasonable pluralism," based on views that "overlap in consensus." Easier said than done: doctrines that might be reasonable to some people may obviously be unreasonable to others. And common sense, we know, is sometimes not very helpful is defining reasonableness. How, then, are different groups and people to arbitrate their differences in a setting like this? And who would do this arbitrating? Is it possible, furthermore, to derive a politics of difference in city life that is reasonable to all?

In Granby, where no conception of legitimate compromise could be established, infighting spelled a long stalemate. Diverse demands and vested interests prevented local groups from working out an integrated neighborhood program. They failed to pinpoint commonality within their own differences. Nor were these groups willing to be forced by the council and housing associations into a commonality that some locals saw as "reasonable" while others saw it as "unreasonable." In the absence of common ground, local groups, residents, and community organizations locked horns with the city council and housing associations.

Given its perennial budget problems, the council's parameters for maneuver were relatively narrow. Budget restraints are one of the unfortunate legacies of the Militant years: Militant's house-building program came at enormous cost, politically as well as financially. The Swiss and Japanese bank loans they received in the mid-1980s left the city with a £750 million debt that is still being paid off. This debt burden has significantly constrained fiscal policy ever since. But even without this burden of debt, on another level we encounter here the limitations of the redistributive paradigm. For once institutional and bureaucratic decision making is placed within a broader political-economic context, we recognize how local state budget is constrained by central government's powers to redistribute national-level revenue. That's presumably why Iris Marion Young says, in *Justice and the Politics of Difference*, that "social justice involving equality among groups who recognize and affirm one another in their specificity can best be realized in our society through large regional governments with mechanisms for representing immediate neighborhoods and towns."[12] Yet in Britain during the past twenty years this logic has been greeted with the obverse ideal. Political power of municipal councils has been eroded by ever more centralized and unaccountable Tory and, more recently, "New Labour" central governments, which have often sought actively to deter local participation and regional democracy.

In Granby's Triangle, there was major disagreement over whether redevelopment should build afresh or rehabilitate old housing stock. As there was a finite amount of public money available, the council wanted to push for the former: it was neater, they said, more efficient and cheaper in the long run. This urban renewal line, of course, seduced a lot of planning authorities on both sides of the Atlantic during the late 1960s and 1970s. In Granby, in the mid-1990s, the policy was viewed suspiciously; some called it "well-intentioned liberalism." The plan to tear down around seven hundred properties and build anew was generally unpopular, but opinion seemed divided. Despite the colossal deprivation—or maybe because of it—people felt bonded to their homes and to their neighborhood, and some were unwilling to move from either. Nevertheless, a ballot initiated by the city council indicated that 80 percent of residents favored demolition and new building redevelopment. But the ballot was attacked by Anna Minter, secretary of the Granby Residents' Association, who suggested that residents were intimidated by the council and housing associations into agreeing to the demolition proposals. She claimed the "majority of people making this type of complaint are elderly, disabled, or non-English speaking."

Some residents felt neglect in Granby had been deliberately deployed to get people out. Gentrification and "ethnic cleansing" were other accusations. Even though the city council fiercely denied these claims, there have been hints of a cleanup in Granby. Accentuating the rift between black and white Toxteth is the Mother and Baby Hospital, a major component of Project Rosemary, an ongoing £60 million public-private partnership between Liverpool city council, the Cathedral Estates Project, Merseyside Task Force, local housing associations, and private developers. In the hospital's shadow is Minster Court, a luxury upper-income, gated apartment complex, a stone's throw away from the University of Liverpool's campus. Immediately across the Upper Parliament Street borderline, it's another story. Here, the city council has been attacked for its appalling maintenance and street cleaning record. Garbage is often uncollected for weeks on end, curb crawling and prostitution are late-night regulars, and street lighting is dim and frequently fails; darkened sidewalks become even more menacing for innocent pedestrians. Many avoid them after dark. Council officials appear aware of their own failings. Alistair McDonald at the council claimed that the Granby scheme has been "hanging there for two to three years. There's a need to clear the air. [The issue] hasn't been brilliantly handled. . . . [But] there's a deep discontent within the community"[13]

Compromise over how to proceed has been hampered, in the first instance, by conflict between different tenure groups—owner-occupiers, private renters, housing association tenants, and council tenants, each of whom have mutually exclusive interests at stake. Such a state of affairs is itself a kind of "politics of difference," since each tenure group expresses a particular partial standpoint, throwing up thorny questions about redistributive justice and fairness in the city. A familiar renter grumble was that "selfish owner-occupiers want to spoil it for everyone else." The Granby Residents' Association, established back in 1992 at the time of the initial consultation exercise in Granby, was probably the most vociferous community group in the area. It lobbied for owner-occupier interests. Thus, said Elaine Stewart, a senior officer in the council's Housing and Consumer Services Directorate, "it isn't representative of popular opinion in Granby." On the other hand, Anna Minter of Granby Residents' Association was adamant that the council and housing associations have employed "underhanded tactics," being "hell-bent" on destroying the neighborhood. Should the proposed block-by-block demolition take place, market rates for houses in Granby spelled minimal compensation and prefigured problems with re-purchasing. A lot of houses in the neighborhood are worth only between £8,000 and £20,000. The Residents' Association, accordingly, began to spearhead GRAD—Granby Residents Against Demolition. But hearsay claimed that many people were afraid to speak frankly at street meetings; they've only reluctantly supported anti-demolition motions. And the South Granby Residents' Association, a mix of tenants and owner-occupiers, are apparently pro-development, via gradual, not wholesale, demolition.

Meanwhile, writ large in the area has been highly emotive sentiment like: "This does not concern you as a white man, we're doing this for the black community."[14] Such a remark implied that Granby's problems were, above all, black problems, solvable only by local black people themselves—suggesting complications went beyond mere vested housing interests. Certainly, tenure itself gets embroiled in issues like length of residence, ethnic status, and unevenness in power relations between particular local groups, between blacks and whites, and within blacks and whites. Figures show that blacks in Toxteth are nearly three times as likely to be housing association tenants as whites (21.4 percent compared with 8.2 percent). Numbers are comparable for council tenancy: around 22.3 percent and 28.8 percent for blacks and whites respectively. By the same token, to speak simply in terms of an exclusively "black" issue in Granby needs to be framed against two immediate caveats.

First of all, there has been antagonism between Liverpool-born and older established blacks and newly arrived non-English-speaking immigrants over housing allocation. Somalis especially, who number a couple of thousand in Liverpool, find themselves frequent targets of abuse. While Liverpool has a long-established Somali population, over the last decade this has grown with the influx of newer immigrants fleeing domestic civil war. By all accounts, these people have gained, and are gaining, fast-track entry into the area's housing and social services. This has sparked resentment from longer-standing black peoples who feel Somalis receive preferential treatment. As such, local black interests aren't monolithic or unified: they're heterogeneous and usually internally acrimonious. Of course, this is what makes Toxteth cultural life so vibrant and rich yet makes its politics so frustrating and angry. Antagonism does exist between different black groups in Toxteth, particularly when communities compete for limited welfare resources. This fact underscores, too, how bottom-line economic pressures inevitably wedge into, constrain, and reshape expressions of identity and single-issue politics.

The second point to heed emerges from the 1991 Census for Liverpool. Even allowing for the plausible belief that the census understates the city's black population (and that its mixed-race hybridity makes ethnic categorization notoriously difficult), it's nonetheless clear the bulk of Granby's 13,000 or so residents are in fact poor whites. The Census records ethnic minorities (i.e. Black Caribbean, Black African, Black Other, Chinese, Other Asian, and Other) as forming 27.7 percent of the overall ward population. (For Liverpool overall, 3.7 percent are officially classified as black or ethnic minority, around 17,000 people, of whom approximately 7,000 reside in Abercromby, Arundel, and Granby.) In other words, many of the 70 percent-odd indigent whites in Granby are fellow sufferers and hence potential allies in their fight for justice. True, black poverty is often generated by a whole set of different structural and ideological forces than white poverty. But, at the same time, blacks and whites surely have common demands to decent housing, schooling, and quality of life, and to a future that goes beyond mere survival.

Toxteth's multicultural social landscape has generated a lot of different sorts of activism and political expression. Ironically, this might be as much a stumbling block as a virtue. The 1980s were a big political awakening for black and minority groups in Toxteth, and community groups have flourished since then. There are over sixty community groups, ethnic societies, and associations listed in Liverpool 8 alone. Here's a sample: Merseyside Caribbean Center, Women's Refuge, East African Welfare Association, Ghana Women's Association, Liverpool Black Sisters, Islamic Cultural Center, Merseyside Immigration Advice Unit, Merseyside Somali Association, Nigerian National Union, Pakistan Center, Rialto Neighborhood Council, Merseyside Black HIV/AIDS Forum, Weller Street Cooperative, Granby Drugs Awareness Project, Liverpool Muslim Society, Steve Biko Housing Association, Ponsonby Neighborhood Center, Freedom of Choice Housing Co-op, and Barbados

Health Group. These groups are frequently single issue and rally around many different themes, ranging from nationalism and identity politics to gender, residency issues, and religious affiliation.

The politics of each group is seldom clearly defined; often it's ambiguous. Moreover, the only attribute that's muted and garbled here is perhaps class. Paradoxically, if these groups have anything in common then it's the common trait of poverty; they're all members of the working class, they all have to sell their labor power as a commodity to make ends meet. While some of the area's cooperatives and housing groups do advocate working class–based initiatives, these tend toward an "inward" kind of class consciousness; rarely does it reach out beyond the neighborhood's immediate low-income housing concerns. (The archetypal paradigm here is found at the Eldonian's Housing Co-op in Vauxhall, overlooking the docklands, several miles north of Toxteth. At the Eldonian's, we find a closed, Labour-voting, working-class Catholic community, whose protagonists comprise ex-workers from the Tate and Lyle sugar plant; the co-op now stands on the plant's old site. Still, despite the Eldonian's impressive material and political gains, their model isn't instructive in a multicultural environment.)

Perhaps there's sound reasoning behind this paradoxical aversion to questions of class in Toxteth. For in the past class politics in Liverpool have always been conducted under the umbrella of the local Labour Party. But nowadays many working-class blacks reach out for representation via alternative means, invariably along racial, national, or gender-based kinship contours. In this regard, the mid-1980s' fiasco of Militant enters the fray. The wounds inflicted by Militant's anti-affirmative action, and its antics over the Sam Bond affair, have yet to heal; they're still painful for a lot of the city's black population. The local Labour Party and Liverpool's city council has a record on race relations that is less than glowing. Of the city council's 30,000 workforce (Liverpool's biggest employer), only a tiny percentage of ethnic minorities are evident. In 1989, the Commission for Racial Equality (CRE) issued to the Labour council a "nondiscrimination notice" in connection with its housing allocation policies. The notice recommended a monitoring of ethnic minority housing allocation. Although the nondiscrimination notice ended in 1994, and Liberals have subsequently seized control of the city, black groups in Toxteth remain leery of both city council and local Labour Party politics. The upshot is that explicit questions of class have tended to disappear from local black and ethnic organizing agendas. Any future class politics in Granby would have to be more flexible, much less rigidly party-oriented, much less boss-based patronage.

Compromise has never been a prominent feature of left politics in Liverpool. Nonetheless, there has been some attempt to coordinate frequently disparate community groups in Toxteth, many of whom fall apart almost as quickly as they come together, especially as they struggle to eke out precious funding. The Princes Park Community Council is such an umbrella organization, one of two community councils left in Liverpool. Partly funded by the city council, it meets once a month and is made up of those delegates from area-wide community organizations. Not all Toxteth community groups particpate, however, leading to dislocation and prioritization of the affairs raised by more vocal groups. To that degree, the difficulty more generally is how, when different groups are forced to confront structures of power in their neighborhoods, can single-issue agendas be affirmed when they coexist with commonly agreed district strategies? How, in other words, can single-issue groups make connections with other groups within an openly unified organization? And this without their respective agendas being either depoliticized entirely or else subsumed under a party political canvas.

Failing that, in the absence of any effective forum for debate and negotiation to establish commonality or to promote empathy—in the absence of what Jürgen Habermas calls "intersubjective communication"—fragmentation of these different marginal voices seems inevitable. Fragmentation and particularity, without cement or universality, means voices will resound in the political twilight zone: people bawl, but they're ignorant of anybody else. People and groups, at that point, seal themselves off from a potentially progressive and reasonable accord and resist any "overlapping consensus." This, in turn, militates against their chances of survival as a locally active and recognized community group. Rawls's veil of ignorance remains literally that: ignorance, an incapacity to move beyond their own "original position."

There are hints that this sort of compartmentalization has occurred in Toxteth. This situation is quite apparent in Granby, where the proposed redevelopment plan accentuated the need for an agreed notion of "reasonable commonality." Of course, in contemporary urban theory appeals for commonality sound unfashionable in the light of postmodern celebrations of "otherness." But when assorted ruling classes force people to consume themselves in the visceral wreckage of inner-city life, and where the poor are subordinated and often placed in zero-sum situations, commonality and togetherness in struggle has to be a prerequisite for any meaningful minority politics. But it can't be achieved in Toxteth by identifying oneself in purely separatist terms. First of all, it fails to recognize the ambiguity and rich commingling of the area's heritage. Second, it creates an artificial border around the contact zones of different communities in the neighborhood, preventing a potentially creative porosity between people who might look different, act different, and who might not understand one another, but who nevertheless share a common culture and experience. Community activists and anti-racists in the area desperately need to mobilize around this reasoning. Digging out "city trenches," to use Ira Katznelson's telling phrase, around strictly racial or single-issue battle lines makes it tough to forge a transformative politics that gets to the heart of local job creation, racism, crime, drug addiction, lousy housing, and run-down schools and parks.

The pursuit for common agreement involves negotiation within local communities themselves. Then they can pit their wits against "external" forces. In real-life urban politics this is inevitably a messy and tedious business. In Toxteth, common and consensual agreement is vital as the first tentative step toward the formulation of longer-term regeneration, not just of housing but of economic and cultural development, of local political empowerment. Meantime, unless communities recognize one another's plight within a common standard of justice, disagreement and internal conflict translates itself into inaction. Maybe the lesson that Granby's redevelopment can teach those concerned about struggling for social justice in the city is that difference has to be affirmed while holding on to some mutually agreed definition of commonality. Otherwise there's no practical way forward. Class could be that cement, that unity in difference, if only the cracks can overlap.

FROM THE POLITICS OF DIFFERENCE
TO DIFFERENT POLITICS (AND BACK AGAIN)

The precarious divide between the politics of militant separatism and the politics of difference voiced within a common frame of reference is something Iris Marion Young has tried to pinpoint. In *Justice and the Politics of Difference*, she tries to maximize cultural heterogeneity and social group difference while minimizing its potential separatist pathologies. Her vision of a progressive "politics of difference" redefines the notion of justice, moving it away from the influential Rawlsian ideal, as laid out in *A Theory of Justice*. Young indicts Rawls for his exclusive prioritization of distribution, his hollow abstract universality, an a priori assumption of an alike public, and an insensitivity to real-life context. In response to such criticism, Rawls has reevaluated his classic work on the basic features of a fair society, changing tack somewhat to embrace a little of Young's revisionism. In *Political Liberalism,* he redefines a "well-ordered society." Now, the relatively homogeneous society united in its basic moral beliefs—as posited in *Theory*—is no longer recognized as viable. Instead, Rawls views a democratic society as "a plurality of reasonable yet incompatible comprehensive doctrines."[15] "Reasonable pluralism," Rawls now admits, "shows that, as used in *Theory*, the idea of a well-ordered society of justice as fairness is unrealistic." Reasonableness, more specifically, covers the "major religious, philosophical, and moral aspects of human life. . . . and organizes and characterizes recognized values so that they are compatible with one another and express an intelligible view of the world."[16] Says Rawls, "Reasonable persons see that the burdens of judgment set limits on what can be reasonably justified to others, and so they endorse some form of liberty of conscience and freedom of thought." At the same time, it's "unreasonable for us to use political power, should we possess it, or share it with others, to repress comprehensive views that are not unreasonable."[17]

Rawls's appeal for a reasonable pluralism doesn't have to be as woolly as it sounds, nor is it entirely incompatible with Young's own normative politics of difference. After all, when people are excluded from active political participation in urban affairs, distributional needs are all that remains for communities and groups to organize around and seek representation. It's within this political context that dialogue and conflict doubtless ensues, and it's one where a "politics of difference" might begin to get constructed. Here questions of what are "reasonable" and "fair" might likewise enter debate—even if, as Rawls says, they are always worked out behind the "veil of ignorance." Interestingly, the urban planner Susan Fainstein reckons that there might be a hidden Marxist inflection in all this. Indeed, she claims that David

Harvey's ethical propositions in *Social Justice and the City* implicitly accept the Rawlsian justice-as-fairness principle.[18] This poses certain problems, she argues, because it affirms a moral standpoint that is generally treated with suspicion by Marxists. If Fainstein is right, it suggests that Harvey is unable to supplant so unequivocally the liberal formulations, expressed in Part I of *Social Justice*, with any Marxist counterpart. Maybe the toughest challenge, both theoretically and practically, is how to link up race, ethnicity, and identity—questions revolving around themes of oppression and domination—with political-economic over redistributive justice, without the latter undermining the constitutive qualities of the former.

Part of the dilemma in making this ideal actual is simple human fallibility. Each of us, as Salman Rushdie has pointed out, is "obliged to accept that [we are] part of the crowd, part of the ocean, part of the storm, so that objectivity becomes a great dream, like perfection, an unattainable goal for which one must struggle in spite of the impossibility of success."[19] Sometimes, such is the enormity of getting by, of just surviving, that empathy is the last thing anyone can visualize. That there's really "just us" may be the only immediate reality.[20] It might also be the only practical line to take to radicalize for just desserts. The experience of inferiority and oppressed status does indeed prompt feelings of isolation and a recognition that, maybe, there is only "just us" against the powerful structures of injustice and domination. Similarly, it's hard to see how anything can be won for dispossessed groups in a society based upon inequality and unreasonableness that doesn't require standing on somebody else's toes. That said, a "just us" sentiment that prioritizes an ontological essentialism, rather than a strategic essentialism, is always destined to lead to isolation and ostracism in the long run. For it's not a politics of difference, but a different politics: it's a different politics because it sees no one, embraces no one, empathizes with no one. Meanwhile, no one listens, least of all the ruling classes, who are adept at creating separatism, and who prosper from it.

Battling against this limited and limiting politics requires some forum for listening to different voices so that the terrain of debate and negotiation can be broadened and where competing voices can be reasonably judged. Social policy and urban planning, as initiated through state institutions, must be pressured and sensitized to such a requirement. Usually this pressure comes from below, up from the street, from demonstrations, from marches as much as ballet boxes. Inevitably, too, this progressive politics will doubtless focus upon distributive issues—political-economic issues—but it will have to be so much more, too, as the deadlock at Granby showed. Only then can the ground be cleared for an imaginative alternative that is not perpetual "just us" strife nor tyrannical imposition, where what is reasonable is defined simply as what benefits the powerful and can be shoved down the throats of the powerless in an unreasonable manner. Thus the different politics affirmed by needy people has to be incorporated into a politics of difference that is galvanized into some form of democratic citizenship. In any event, we can follow Michael Walzer's reasoning that "tumult is better than passivity; shared purposes (even when we don't approve) are better than private listlessness."[21]

But let's get real here: as we've witnessed, even getting people who are different to talk about compromise proved a veritable stumbling block in Toxteth. The inaction over regenerating Granby seems not only a missed opportunity in economic terms; it equally misses a great chance to radicalize and yoke different communities. This affects the future trajectory of Toxteth more generally. Indeed, there is such a vast array of activism and activists there, in the shape of different community groups, resident associations, and ethnic identity and lifestyle support networks, that a pretty hefty alliance might one day be in the offing—if these groups can be brought together. The quest of bringing oppressed people together has more general currency. For it's almost impossible to achieve a democratic, nonexclusionary urbanism without recourse to some standard of universality, a value that is nonreducible and applies to all. Words come easy, but realistic execution, in real places, in real cities, with real complex and contradictory and ignorant and torn people, is something else again.

Salman Rushdie states the basic difficulty in the way of establishing such standards of universality: "Human beings do not perceive things whole; we are not gods but wounded creatures, cracked lenses, capable only of fractured perceptions. Partial beings, in all the senses of the phrase. Meaning is a shaky edifice we build out of scraps, dogmas, childhood injuries, newspaper articles, chance remarks, old films, small victories, people hated, people loved; perhaps it is because our sense of what is the case is constructed from such inadequate materials that we defend it so fiercely, even to the death."[22] That we are wounded creatures suggests that finding ideas that do bind us is all the more crucial. This is especially so in our cities where meaning is indeed a "shaky edifice." In the end, the shaky edifice is what makes city life so wonderfully exciting, yet at the same time so precarious and fragile. The fin-de-millénaire city poses new dilemmas, new hazards for neighborhoods, for people everywhere and everyday. Each of us somehow holds fractured perceptions, views things through cracked mirrors; we have little choice but to do otherwise. Everybody experiences fusions and fissions in our lives, and negotiating these fusions and fissions is a daunting prospect for city people. The big question is how can we celebrate fission while becoming solid citizens.

4

The Urbanization of Labor: Living Wage Activism in Los Angeles

For well over a decade now, U.S. cities have been locked into a mode of urbanization best described as entrepreneurial. During the 1980s and 1990s, whole cities assumed the status of enterprises and became very adept at enhancing a "good business climate" reputation, hustling inexorably to the tune of the bottom line. Indeed, creating and re-creating healthy business climates has apparently been vital not only for the growth and continued financial viability of cities but also for their survival, and the survival of every city in an age of global insecurity and competitive volatility.[1] Apologists and gurus of such a line have set the tone of recent debate about the nature of contemporary urbanism and the trajectory of urban development.[2] For these people there's simply no alternative to the entrepreneurial paradigm. Now, the argument goes, ubiquitous capital deregulation and corporate hypermobility browbeats and cajoles cities into capturing a piece of the action. If cities don't capture a piece of the action, then apparently this action—that is, the investment, jobs, industries, the well-heeled consumers—will go elsewhere, to another town, maybe close by, or to somewhere where the package is more favorable, more profitable, more efficient in serving the needs of capitalism. Accordingly, mayors, local councillors, chambers of commerce, and business elites have come together to work out their own growth strategy, one where the public sector lends something of a visible hand, absorbing part of the market risk, thus helping locales become more economically attractive, more attuned to daring and entrepreneurship.

Here, a lot of heady legal, political, and economic mechanisms have been deployed to push things along. For a time, Urban Development Action Grants (UDAGs) were the preferred mechanism. These interest-free leverage grants, bestowed upon intrepid developers, were supposed to help regenerate run-down areas, provide jobs, rekindle local economies, kick-start small businesses, and attract investors to spaces and projects that might otherwise be shunned. During the 1980s, New York, Detroit, and Baltimore topped the national UDAG league. But few strict guidelines were set about what these handouts should be used for. So rather than fund low-income housing or other social infrastructure, UDAGs sponsored the construction of convention centers, hotels, marinas, and expensive residential complexes. Soon they were hastening, not ameliorating, social polarization inasmuch as few of the goodies seemed to trickle down to needy people. After awhile, UDAGs became the greatest hotel-building venture in American history. And, if that wasn't enough, the new hotels barely paid employees minimum wage; large chains like Marriott and Hyatt also turned into big time union busters.

The "empowerment zones" set up by President Clinton in 1993 merely continued the trend whereby the public sector underwrote corporate interests. Specific areas in cities were gerrymandered into zones that waived property taxes and ensured that locating companies received income tax credits for each new person they hired. Meanwhile, more direct support for companies came in the shape of Industrial Development Bonds (IDBs)—federally sponsored bonds whose earnings directly accrued to the specific business—and Tax Increment Financing Districts, yet another form of corporate welfare. Citizens for Tax Justice estimate that lost revenue from the IDB program alone between 1996 and 2000 weighed in at around $900 million, which is more than the total federal budget for urban mass transit.[3]

Policies like this pretty much follow neoliberal, supply-side economic formulae, nostrums cherished by both Reagan and George Bush Sr. as economic *and* urban orthodoxies; the link between economic growth and the urban process assumes an inextricable unity. To that degree, there has been a decisive correlation between Clinton's so-called New

Economy and the dynamics of American urbanization. In other words, there's a complex spatial logic and spatial texturing to global and U.S. business cycles. Throughout the second half of the 1990s especially, there's been a new building boom and reconfiguration of city space up and down the metropolitan hierarchy, fueled by a buoyant economy and shamelessly bullish financial sector. One of its most contradictory motifs, now coming to the fore rather too palpably for most people, is surging property prices (and rents) coupled with stagnating and shrinking household incomes. Rents go up, and landlords and developers make a killing; wages take a dip, worker insecurity grows and family tensions intensify. All of which is supposed to signify prosperous times, good business climate conditions. Until recently, it has dramatized the form and functioning of urban (and suburban) America.

This neoliberal model of the city was relatively unchallenged in the United States for much of the '80s and '90s. It continues its dominance in the corridors of power, where millionaire investors are still heartily welcome. Since the mid-'90s, ordinary working people have begun to fight back and to regain some of the ground they had lost in a previously one-sided class war. This radical thrust from the grass roots has created a new item in the political vocabulary of the American city: "living wage" campaigns.

These campaigns are beginning to contest rampant subsidy abuse, as well as the unaccountable squandering of public monies. They are currently making a lot of noise in American cities and are gathering strength fast, demanding a new innovative growth-with-equity urbanization paradigm. They're doing this when the number of people and families living below the poverty line in U.S. cities is increasing, when the gap between rich and poor is widening, and when the standard of living for working people is eroding; they're doing this, too, when in California, the nation's richest state and world's seventh- largest economy, nearly one in five people are living below the poverty line; and they're doing this when the lack of decent-paying jobs isn't merely a localized affair, either. Throughout the United States there are growing numbers of people in work, but work doesn't enable them to make ends meet. Even during the boom years of the 1990s, the bulk of the nation's needy were actually working people, those who had jobs, maybe even full-time jobs, maybe even jobs with lots of overtime. But those jobs didn't pay an adequate wage nor have health benefits.

In this chapter, I want to explore living wage activism more closely. I want to suggest that the living wage struggle is helping to forge a new kind of urban process. Now, the circulation of surplus value is being rechanneled away from the "urbanization of capital" toward the "urbanization of labor," toward a city more sensitive to the needs of its workers rather than its investors. Although living wage campaigns are sweeping across the United States, and already made law in cities as diverse as Baltimore, Boston, Dayton, Duluth, Durham, Jersey City, Minneapolis–Saint Paul, Milwaukee, New Haven, Oakland, and Portland, I specifically want to focus on the struggle that has been growing in Los Angeles. This city provides a fascinating glimpse of how a multihued population has managed to unite around the wage relation. Here, community and church groups have joined hands with emerging militant unions like the Services Employees International Union (SEIU) and the Hotel Employees and Restaurant Employees (HERE) in a genuine gesture of class solidarity and struggle. They've found common ground in a city infamously divided by racial hate and fear. And although the coalition's successes in pushing through living wage legislation remains uneven and fairly narrow in scope—covering only 8,000 or so workers—it has nonetheless given communities and labor in the city new tools to work with, especially tools for building a more wide-reaching social movement. In this way, all living wage struggles signal a new beginning. They now offer progressives everywhere a big new urban idea from below at a time when the only big ideas that matter have come from above.

FROM THE BONAVENTURE TO AN ORGANIZING VENTURE: THE LOS ANGELES LIVING WAGE COALITION

The prehistory of the Hotel Employees and Restaurant Employees (HERE) Local 11—the union representing housekeepers, porters, busboys, dishwashers, and food servers, and a prime mover and shaker today in L.A.'s living wage rumbles—makes sordid reading for leftists. Pre-1989, before Maria-Elena Durazo took charge, the local was nothing more than a corrupt, top-down, white, old guard irrelevance; none of its meetings in the early 1980s were ever translated into Spanish; union leaders had no idea how to respond to the massive changes affecting the city's hotel and restaurant trade, when market forces ran rampant and employer-engineered decertification seemed unstoppable: L.A.'s $8 billion tourist industry was developing off the backs of an ever-expanding low-wage Latino workforce who had nowhere to turn. That was until Durazo entered the fray. Soon she cleaned up the local, revamped it, made it multilingual, confrontational, subversive, and showed how its predominantly immigrant membership might organize themselves. A lot of Latino activists, formerly involved in the California farmworkers' struggle during the previous decade, closed ranks alongside Local 11's new leader. "We had learned how to organize immigrant workers around issues of class and justice," Durazo said. "We were doing that again." Her sustained campaign managed to inspire members, reached out for new recruits, trained potential organizers inside the swanky hotels, and organized high-profile direct actions all over the city. A new union militancy and empowerment process began to flourish. Durazo was employing Sweeneyesque reforms six years before their time; maybe it has been more reminiscent of the old CIO in its 1930s glory days.

Local 11 has since grown into a formidable energizing and radical force. Curiously, at the same time as radical academics and cultural critics were busy deconstructing L.A.'s Bonaventure Hotel as an icon of late capitalist postmodernity, Durazo and her crew were trying to reconstruct the union there.[4] For a while, they'd been fighting for a livable wage—a fair day's pay for a fair day's work—and were getting it inside luxury hotels like the Bonaventure, where their members had been scrubbing bathtubs and toilets, making beds, waiting tables, and dumping garbage for a pittance. To dramatize their plight, Local 11 employed disciplined yet highly inventive media and street tactics. Gone, for example, was the formal stationary workplace picket line. Instead, members held lobby sit-ins, became human billboards, staged mass boycotts and flying pickets and leafleting initiatives, and demonstrated raucously on the street. Other activism was more theatrical, like the so-called coffee-ins or "Java for Justice," where Local 11 members took over whole dining rooms of hotels and ordered coffee all around. Clerics sometimes lent a hand, giving short homilies about social justice to bemused diners and hotel guests. Local 11 became what Mike Davis called a "peaceful guerrilla army," and their members spoke of "building not just a union but a social movement, like those of the 1930s and 1960s."[5]

In the wake of the 1992 riots, the union also produced a controversial video: *City on the Edge*. Hundreds of copies were mailed all over the country to prospective convention center planners and business investors. Those who actually put the thing into their VCR would have watched the awful truth: more trouble would follow in L.A. soon, unless the city's low-wage service sector, underwritten by hotel employers' union-busting tactics, didn't receive significant pay hikes. Not surprisingly, the hometown business community and then incumbent Mayor Tom Bradley were livid; Peter Ueberroth's Rebuilding L.A. Committee was none too pleased, either. At that time some of the big hotels like the Westin Bonaventure, Biltmore, Los Angeles Hilton, Century Plaza, and Hyatt Wilshire actively averted union negotiations. As longtime L.A. activist Eric Mann emphasized in his defense of Local 11's video, the pro-business Los Angeles Hotel Employers Association was even engineering a two-year wage freeze for their workforce.[6] Yet the video's portrayal of what Mann called "Greed on the Edge" nonetheless shook people up. With its graphic images—a little like those of Rodney King—it showed a society gone terribly awry and in desperate need of repair.

By late 1995, Local 11's campaign broadened as a small group of community activists, organized labor, lawyers, and church groups came together to gather information on the successful living wage campaign in Baltimore in December 1994. Baltimore's campaign served as a prototype when its Ordinance 442 mandated a minimum hourly wage, effective as of July 1995, of $6.10 for anyone working on a city service contract. This would increase to $6.60 the following year, reaching $7.70 by 1998, thereby lifting a family of four above the poverty line. Spearheading the campaign was the Solidarity Sponsoring Committee (SSC), a group of low-income city service workers, a lot of them African-American, and Baltimoreans United in Leadership Development (BUILD). The American Federation of State, County, and Municipal Employees (AFSCME) gave added labor muscle to this robust, coalition-based grassroots struggle. Church leaders in Baltimore had witnessed a sharp rise in the number of working people relying on social service agencies for food and housing. A lot of poor families, they realized, were low-wage earners not welfare recipients. BUILD reckoned that poverty-wage jobs spawned directly because of the subsidized redevelopment of downtown and the contracting-out of much city service work. But under the new ordinance, about 4,000 janitors, food service employees, laborers, machine cleaners and repairmen, stenographers, carpet cleaners, bus drivers—many hitherto making bare minimum rates—benefited from significant wage hikes.

In Los Angeles, the new grassroots conglomerate began exploring the possibilities of engaging in a similar venture. Before long, the fledgling organization—the Los Angeles Living Wage Coalition—began gaining grants from voluntary foundations, labor unions, and several religious associations. These religious associations developed into an interfaith organization called CLUE (Clergy and Laity United for Economic Justice). Working within the coalition, CLUE takes inspiration from the Old Testament Book of Deuteronomy (24:14): "You shall not withhold the wages of poor and needy laborers, whether other Israelites or aliens who reside in your land in one of your towns."

As the coalition generated steam, drew in kindred spirits, and gathered momentum and confidence, it developed as one crucial arm of a bigger umbrella concern called LAANE (Los Angeles Alliance for a New Economy), whose executive director is Madeline Janis-Aparicio, an attorney and experienced lobbyist and organizer. LAANE employs twelve full-time staff and now takes up one whole floor of a shabby Beaux Arts office building right in the heart of downtown's jewelry district. LAANE itself is an offshoot of the earlier Tourism Industry Development Council (TIDC), another brainchild of Janis-Aparicio, back in 1993, which received funding sponsorship from HERE Local 11. Harold Meyerson, *L.A. Weekly*'s veteran labor commentator, reckons that LAANE "has become one of the most important forces—and surely the most innovative—for social justice in L.A."[7] Under LAANE's auspices, says Meyerson, L.A. labor relations are moving along on to terra nova. Indeed, the organization has been instrumental in the collective bargaining for thousands of low-wage workers, the bulk of whom are Latino, while it's played hardball with L.A.'s conservative booster coalition about a growth-with-equity development vision. As new shopping malls, convention centers, theme parks, and hotels mushroom or get touted, and as the subsidies and low-interest loans get doled out by the institutions like the Community Redevelopment Agency (CRA), LAANE wants decent-paying jobs for those who'll be cleaning and servicing them.

HERE Local 11 also sought to extend its advocacy for a living wage for other low-wage earners in L.A.'s hotels. In late 1997, it was involved in negotiations with fourteen hotels for a new pay and benefits contract that would guarantee wage increases from the existing $8.15 an hour to $11.05 over a six-year period. Agreement was initially reached with six big hotels—the Biltmore, Hyatt Regency, Omni, Holiday Inn Convention Center, West Hollywood's Sunset Hyatt, and the Sheraton Universal. Downtown, all the union hotels besides the Bonaventure have complied. On the west side, the Beverly Wilshire, Beverly Hilton, and some other glitzy hotels have yet to sign the deal.[8] In any event, this new contract is already significant, for it creates what Local 11 staffer James Elmendorf deems "a new standard for service-sector work in Los Angeles." It forbids signatory hotels from subcontracting work to cheaper nonunion alternatives, and it incorporates new, far-reaching immigrant labor protection clauses: anybody discharged because of suspect or nonexistent immigration papers will have his or her job held over for one year to have time to sort out the problem. "This contract," Maria-Elena Durazo reminded everybody afterward, "didn't fall from the sky. The key to winning was members' involvement in our organizing activity, our political activity."

It was activity of this nature, doggedly organized and bravely practiced, that culminated on March 18, 1997, in the enactment of a living wage ordinance by the Los Angeles city council. A large crowd of supporters cheered when the council voted unanimously, 12–0, to adopt a living wage ordinance. "Extending a hand to thousands of impoverished workers while tossing the mayor a sharp political challenge," said next day's *Los Angeles Times*, the council gave the thumbs up to "an ordinance requiring some private firms with city ties to boost the pay and benefits of their bottom-rung service employees."[9] But the lopsided nature of this vote belied months-long debate, protracted and bitterly contested squabbles, in which business boosterists and the Republican mayor, Richard Riordan, pitted their money and wits against council progressives—notably Jackie Goldberg, a former '60s radical—and Living Wage Coalition activists like Madeline Janis-Aparicio. And the battle was far from done. Indeed, almost before the cheers died down, Riordan vowed to veto the ordinance. "The ordinance," he insisted, "is a step in the wrong direction and undermines our effort to create quality jobs throughout the city." Not unexpectedly, businesses immediately rallied around their multimillionaire mayor. Chamber of Commerce president Ezunial Burts called Riordan's motion "a courageous action," adding "it was right on target."[10] Meanwhile, Noelia Rodriguez, the mayor's press secretary, claimed the measure is "in essence, an additional tax on businesses."

These objections were nevertheless quashed. Several days later, Riordan's veto was overruled, 11–1. "The mayor argued his position," said an elated Janis-Aparicio. "He lost." Enshrined in law henceforth was Living Wage Ordinance (LWO) no. 171547. This compels employers receiving from the city service contracts of over $25,000 and financial assistance for economic development purposes of more than $100,000 a year, or $1 million in any given year, to pay their workers a living wage: $7.39 per hour with health benefits and $8.64 without. If any employee—any janitor, food service worker, security guard—covered by the LWO receives anything less than $8.64, then they're entitled to a health care plan worth at least $1.25 per hour. The LWO similarly holds for all temporary and part-time contractual employees; it is one small yet symbolically significant step in addressing Los Angeles's real economic crisis, where an estimated 35.7 percent of working adults eke out a poverty wage, and where around 2.2 million people have absolutely no health coverage. The vote was really the culmination of a sustained thrust from below, and this was just the opening salvo. As Goldberg said to jubilant Living Wage Coalition members, "This happened because of you."[11]

JUSTICE FOR JANITORS: "THIS IS WAR!"

Alongside Janis-Aparicio at LAANE and Maria-Elena Durazo of HERE Local 11, prominent organizing roles have been played by Miguel Contreras—Durazo's husband and head of the Los Angeles County Federation of Labor—and Mike Garcia, SEIU Local 1877's president. Each has successfully mobilized living wage campaigns as "entry level" organizing vehicles. Contreras, a former protégé of labor legend and United Farm Workers cofounder Cesar Chavez, orchestrates some 400 unions with a total membership of around 700,000 workers, 18 percent of the county labor force—the nation's largest Central Labor Council after New York's.[12] The Federation demonstrated its extensive clout when it mobilized up and down the state to help thwart then-Governor Pete Wilson's controversial Proposition 226, an initiative that would have effectively barred organized labor from the political process.

Meanwhile, a lot of the successful hell-raising had been adopted by that other living wage stalwart, Local 1877 of the Service Employees

International Union (SEIU). As AFL-CIO president John Sweeney's old union—representing janitorial workers in health care and in government and private sectors—SEIU more generally has spearheaded something of a mini-American labor renaissance in recent years, getting its act together at the top as well as at the bottom. In 1998, SEIU organized around 58,000 new members and spent almost half of its budget on organizing—compared with just 3 percent not so long ago. Back in the 1980s, its power in the building service sector was on a grim downslide, hemorrhaging members and losing strength by the minute. But rather than flee the industry altogether, SEIU orchestrated a fight back and a realignment, plunging into a national organizing drive, moving beyond prescribed National Labor Relations Board (NLRB) site-by-site tactics.

For a start, they took a long, hard look at how employer-employee relationships in the building services had changed. Pre-1980s, everything was done in-house, with building owners hiring their own janitorial crews. Then, janitors may have enjoyed some fringe benefits, reasonable living wages, and were likely to be unionized. Since the mid-1980s, building owners had relied exclusively on cleaning contractors, who had jockeyed with other cleaning contractors. Building owners were united in their efforts to keep costs down by contracting-out. Given that cleaning offices and other premises is extremely labor-intensive, the coercive pressure of competition compelled contractors to push down workers' wages to minimal and subminimal levels. Those cleaning contractors who may have paid well and offered decent benefits would now be quickly eliminated from bidding process once the low-balling union-busting contractors played their card. In effect, "bad" money drove out "good" money. Either way, building owners were forcing their nonunion contractors to pay poverty-wage rates.

To halt this onslaught and imminent debacle, in 1985 SEIU engineered one of the most successful unionizing campaigns in the postwar period: "Justice for Janitors." Kicking off in Pittsburgh, spreading quickly to Denver, and eventually reaching L.A. by 1988, the Justice for Janitors (JfJ) crusade wanted nothing else than to build a mass movement—"ONE INDUSTRY, ONE UNION, ONE CONTRACT." That way, JfJ would try to force different employers and contractors across disparate local labor markets to recognize one union, coordinated centrally yet nurtured and organized locally. Stephen Lerner, former director of SEIU's Building Services Organizing, called JfJ "a war against the employers and the building owners, waged on all fronts, [not] leaving any stone unturned."[13] To begin with, this struggle took hold in L.A.'s downtown area, but soon it started to diffuse elsewhere, both in the city and beyond.

The number of L.A.'s janitorial workers doubled between 1980 and 1990 to 28,800; over half were Central American and Mexican immigrants. Over that same period, union membership dipped 77 percent; and the $12.53 an hour wage package received in 1983 was crunched into a $3.35 minimum by 1988. In the meantime, L.A. had experienced an unprecedented commercial building boom, further capitalized by the subcontracting process and lax property tax legislation. Estimates suggest that by contracting-out cleaning services, L.A.'s building owners benefited from 42 percent cost reductions.[14] In 1979, cleaning one square foot of downtown office space averaged $1.87 a year. In 1982, however, that same square foot was trimmed to $1.74; by 1986, $1.28; as of 1993, it stood at the very lean figure of $1.08. And if that wasn't handy enough, greater and greater work had been extracted from fewer and fewer janitors, relative to the huge increase of space. The typical janitor was soon expected to sweep 45,000 square feet of office space, which is a lot more than he once did on the same shift.

L.A.'s property tax rate helped further lubricate the wheels of commercial expansion and profit bonanza. At 1 percent, it's among the friendliest in the country, much less than in Atlanta, Baltimore, Boston, Chicago, Dallas, New York, Philadelphia, or Washington, D.C. Here, too, Proposition 13, which froze many property taxes at 1975 levels, represents a veritable free meal for commercial real estate developers. Soaring building prices, together with a doubling and in some cases a tripling of land values throughout the late 1980s and 1990s, has meant commercial valuations outpacing actual tax assessments. In fact, if landlords had coughed up their fair share of the tax burden, they'd have paid out an additional $500 million for the 1994 tax year alone. But they haven't. Instead, they've become modern-day robber barons, reaping a colossal booty while driving a lot of working people into serious hardship, eroding civil liberties almost to their heart's content.

Within this context, JfJ began in L.A. under the auspices of Local 399. Since then it's attracted 4,000 new members in one of the nation's most creative, rambunctious, and aggressive organizing campaigns, not only making up for the previous decade's casualties but also making great advances as well. In the city's downtown high-rises, union representation has resurged to an estimated 90 percent; city-wide ranks are up to about 70 percent.[15] Along the way, Local 399 embarrassed countless office landlords and wreaked justifiable havoc by staging boisterous demonstrations: occupying lobbies, chanting and screaming and banging drums, and blocking off major traffic boulevards. With such in-your-face tactics, it's little wonder that these bright red T-shirted activists have been dubbed by the business press as engaging in "zany, obnoxious, and occasionally illegal techniques that seem born more of the burlesque hall than the union hall."[16] This is plainly what it takes these days for some employers to respect and recognize the union.

Many L.A. workers have drawn from their experiences and traditions in El Salvador and Guatemala, where being a union member meant not just getting fired but being fired upon. These Latino and Latina service workers have gone from what Mike Davis calls a "pariah proletariat" to the vanguard of a revitalized West Coast labor movement.[17] Moreover, "la lucha" in the office lobbies, in the restaurants and hotels and casinos, and in the streets, might even be the vocabulary of the American labor movement itself in the new millennium. So Central American janitors have no illusions about things. They have to fight to get their fair share of society's wealth. "This is war!" they proclaim.

JfJ's battle mettle got severely tested when its campaign spread to L.A.'s hitherto nonunionized Century City district. In May 1990, 180 janitors walked out on strike because their employer, International Service Systems (ISS), a Danish multinational cleaning company—known as "Top Trash"—that employed 14,000 people nationwide, and operated in thirteen of Century City's eighteen office blocks, paying their work-force a miserly $4.25 an hour, refused to negotiate a union contract.[18] The dispute quickly escalated into big news. SEIU officials went to Denmark to picket outside ISS's headquarters, and Gus Bevona, the power-ful boss of SEIU's New York Local 32B-32J, pledged support for the Century City rebel janitors, threatening a mass walkout of his 5,000 members. Then, in early June 1990, 400 class-conscious strikers and supporters, marching to the beat of conga drums, stormed Century City office buildings and took over lobbies and traffic thoroughfares. Somebody called the cops, and before long their batons were flailing. Scuffles broke out and the peaceful yet defiant protesters were knocked to the ground; some were arrested; others chased into a subterranean parking lot, where they were brutally beaten and maltreated. Sixteen people suffered broken bones and one Latina had a miscarriage.

The strike generated a lot of emotional support and public outrage, and afterward the police were forced to admit that overzealous officers actually caused the violence.[19] Yet it took another five years before Local 399 was victorious and Century City offices became organized. At last century's end, they were about 90 percent unionized. In the process, janitors' wages rose from $4.25 to $6.80 per hour, and from no health coverage to full family health coverage. No mean feat—even if the wage levels were still nothing to write home about. By 1997, though, Local 399 had merged into one of the largest building service locals in the land; 8,000 janitors, alongside 3,500 others working at various racetracks, sports stadiums, and arenas—at facilities touted by 1980s' boosterists as so vital to urban regeneration—combined to form SEIU's new statewide Local 1877, bringing its membership up to a whopping 20,500.

Mike Garcia, the architect of this reorganization, took over as president and shifted the local's HQ from San Jose to L.A., where 1877 will have enormous weight and reach. "What we're looking for is industrial power," said Garcia. "We have to deal with building services as a whole industry. It's not just a group of small contractors, different in every city. The contractors are often the same."[20] He added, "And the client companies, who the contractors work for, are some of the largest in the world—like Pacific Bell, Chevron, and Southern California Edison. They change cleaning contractors like socks. So the only way to really change conditions, and protect our members, is to have the same set of wages and conditions for everyone." The conditions have to be generalized— one industry, one union and one contract. That way, organization can occur at the rank and file level, in place, while it also gets coordinated and diffused over space—the domain of the footloose employer and corporation—through a representative centralized organizational structure, where it can galvanize other members in different places and in different chapters. Establishing a single, common date for contract renewals, in as broad a geographical area as possible, is one key to prospective success. A uniform deal and expiration date would help even up the battlefield: janitors' unions would thereby negotiate with the same companies, at the same time, in many different cities, pushing for the same pay and benefits for everybody.

SEIU 1877 is also involved in a joint drive with HERE 11 and the Living Wage Coalition to incorporate LAX's 4,000 airport security staff, baggage handlers, pre-board screeners, food service workers, wheelchair helpers and runners, janitors, and parking attendants. "Respect at LAX," launched in June 1998, has intensified its intent to lift these service workers—most of whom receive minimum wages without health coverage—out of the poverty trap.[21] Despite Delta, American, United, and Southwest trawling in $2.8 billion in profits during the first quarter of 1998, they refuse to comply with the ordinance, insisting they're governed by federal rather than city law. The airport saga illustrates how LAANE, the Living Wage Coalition, and reenergized organized labor in L.A. cannot rest on their laurels. Assorted employers and business honchos will be forever on the offensive: battling against unions and living wage drives, intimidating union sympathizers, scheming decertification programs, running "captive audience" sessions, recruiting professional union busters, and generally engaging in an amoral class warfare. "When American workers today try to form a union," *The Nation*'s Marc Cooper reminds us, "they're usually immediately confronted by a half-billion-dollar-a-year industry."[22] Meanwhile, Tom Juravich and Kate Bronfenbrenner have assembled disturbing data on employer opposition to unionization in an essay with a revealing little title, "Preparing for the Worst."[23] The authors say "unions will need to develop a much more aggressive grassroots response to employer opposition if they are going to have any success in a deteriorating. . . . organizing climate."

FROM MINIMUM WAGE TO A LIVING WAGE: THE REASSERTION OF CLASS IN THE AMERICAN CITY

"People are sick of giving millions to corporations and receiving nothing in return," says David Buckley of the Association of Community Organizations for Reform Now (ACORN). "They're sick of working full-time but not being able to support their families." Little wonder that people in urban America have begun organizing and have already started to think and work through alternatives—practical and realistic democratic alternatives. These people knew real wages wouldn't increase without grassroots pressure; and they know that the Democrats have sold liberals out on many promises. For years, minimum wage raises have been debated. In September 1997, amid vigorous opposition, Clinton finally upped it to $5.15. That, many progressives conceded, was helpful. But it was barely a step in the right direction. And it came after years of relative stagnation, of relative decline. Between 1955 and 1969, minimum wage rose 56 percent from $4.27 (in 1995 spending power) to $6.65. However, between 1969 and 1995 it fell back to $4.25 per hour, well below its 1955 level.[24] In 1999, the real value of the minimum wage was 30 percent less than it was in 1968. In current dollars, 1968's minimum was $7.37. Back then as well the economy was much less productive. At $5.15 per hour, somebody who works for fifty weeks pulls in $10,300 per annum. That's a good bit less than the officially designated poverty threshold of $15,843 for a family of four.

Simply put, minimum wage nowadays isn't a living wage; it's certainly no "family wage." To compound things, Clinton's 1996 welfare reform legislation, "ending welfare as we know it," requires the unemployed to work for their benefits. Whatever its virtues about instilling dignity in people, "workfare" really means that there's a huge pool of vulnerable men and women shoved on to the labor market where they can be used to undercut prevailing workers and prevailing wage rates. In essence, workfare must undercut wages: if all those currently on welfare are to be absorbed into the ranks of the contingently employed—as Congress hopes—in states with big welfare populations, like California and New York, wages would need to fall by almost 18 percent.

Wage equations here curiously follow Karl Marx's logic from the last century. Take the "General Law of Capitalist Accumulation," chapter 25 of *Capital,* vol. 1. There Marx stresses how the ready availability of a lot of "partially employed or wholly unemployed" workers regulates "the general movement of wages." A capitalist economy, Marx believed, requires a dispensable "industrial reserve army," a "relative surplus population" as a condition for its own growth, for "expanded accumulation." The system literally feeds off unemployment and irregular employment: it needs to keep wages in check and to maintain profitability, especially in the light of capricious business cycles. A surplus population is, in short, "the lever of capitalistic accumulation."

When the going is good, when capital is accumulating and economies are strong enough to absorb the reserve army, wages may go up, given the increased bargaining power of workers. Yet profits may soon start to get squeezed. Then, capitalists may start to lose a portion of their surplus value, may start to pay out more for labor power—for variable capital. At such point, they might, in contemporary language, downsize, "set free" workers, "lessen the numbers of laborers employed in proportion to the increased production." As a result, Marx said, the "diminution of the variable capital"—the diminution of wages—"corresponds rigidly with the diminution of the numbers of laborers employed." Henceforth, falling wages promote an accelerated rate of accumulation. The "over-work" of those still employed "swells the ranks of the reserve, whilst conversely the greater pressure that the latter by its competition exerts on the former, forces these to submit to overwork and to subjugation under the dictates of capital."

All of which sounds eerily familiar. Indeed, today's "contingent" workers correspond to Marx's *stagnant* and *floating* relative surplus populations; those laborers who get variously repelled from, and attracted to, work, and whose status is wholly uncertain, wholly unstable. They form part of the active labor army, but their employment is extremely irregular and they represent a formidably disposable and flexible kind of labor power. (No surprises that America's largest single employer nowadays is Manpower Inc., the temporary help agency, who rent out 800,000 floating workers each year.) In effect, contingent work has been the lever of expanded accumulation in contemporary climes.[25] It's been integral in the corporate sector's great productivity heist. And it's acted as a *general law* as well, bearing down on working populations across America, enacted and reenacted as a brutal class war, virtually one-sided, that perpetuates and preys off worker insecurity.

A lot of people these days find themselves "set free," tossed out of work, downsized and rightsized and outsourced, downgraded into the ranks of a floating relative surplus population. Maybe some never thought of themselves as Marx's "modern working class," never dreamt they'd one day join the ranks of the partially employed or wholly unemployed, especially because some weren't factory hands nor blue-collar workers, but instead wore suits and were employed in offices or labs or schools or dealing rooms. Yet now they, too, must sell themselves piecemeal, as a commodity, finding work only insofar as their labor is able to create capital for somebody else. Today, few workers are safe; many are at the mercy of market demands and vicissitudes in competition for labor power. This is really what Marx meant by the "working class" and why he saw its ranks growing.[26]

That, too, is presumably why so many different kinds of people, with different kinds of skin color and ethnicities and gender, in many different kinds of cities, in different kinds of work, have been so active in living wage campaigns, and have pulled together in unusual and unexpected ways, thrusting themselves into municipal-level politics and into unionizing drives, often for the first time. For everyone involved, living wage has been a quest for economic justice; it's likewise been taken as morally right, as a just dessert for those who work hard and who are trying to support themselves as well as future generations. Assorted umbrella groups, like the New Party, ACORN, and AFL-CIO, have made living wage drives the mainstay of their recent programs. The New Party and ACORN have excellent living wage websites that keep activists and fellow travelers informed about what's what with living wage campaigns up and down the country; these websites provide information on how people can get involved in struggles in communities near them.[27] The AFL-CIO's "America Needs a Raise" and "Road to a Union City" blitz organizing drives have enabled unions and community to forge closer bonds, broadening and deepening each other's respective agendas.

FROM "LEAN" URBANIZATION TO THE URBANIZATION OF LABOR

Since 1979, more than 43 million jobs have been eliminated and nearly three-quarters of American households have had some kind of close encounter with job layoffs. But as the jobs got eliminated, and downsizing became epidemic, the math became more complicated. For over the same period, paradoxically, there's also been a *net increase* of 27 million jobs, from 90 million in 1979 to 117 million in 1997, easily enough to absorb all laid-off workers. So downsizing isn't a tale of mass unemployment. Actually, about 70 percent of downsized workers eventually find new jobs. But here's the sting—according to U.S. Labor Department statistics only about 35 percent of laid-off workers find jobs that pay the same as their old ones. For most downsizing firms, profits were good. Layoffs, however, were deemed "rational" in the light of "efficiency drives." And efficiency drives, needless to say, sought more profit while trying to stave off *anticipated* business downturns. Cutting the payroll was simply company strategy of *first resort*. As ever, short-term balance sheet dictates call the shots and Wall Street acts as both judge and jury.

And all too often besuited moneymen give the thumbs up to the lean company. When Sears announced 50,000 jobs cut its stock climbed 4 percent; Xerox axed 10,000 jobs and its shares surged 7 percent; in April 1995, Mobil proclaimed their quarterly profits up 19 percent from last year. Next day, they announced a 9 percent boost in dividend pay out to shareholders. A month afterward they said 4,700 jobs had to go, 9.2 percent of the workforce. That same afternoon Mobil's market value traded at $3.88 per share, 4.1 percent more than the previous day's level. Shareholders, and especially CEOs, whose salaries increasingly comprise stock options, thereby reap huge windfall gains. They grow fatter while their workforce grows fewer and leaner, working longer, harder, and faster, usually for less pay and with limited or no health coverage. What characterizes the downsized condition, then, is unheralded job insecurity, falling real wages, and a maldistribution of wealth. The downsized condition in the United States is the condition of the working poor.

Globalization as an international process, and downsizing as a domestic economic condition, have affected American urbanization in telling ways. Job layoffs, diminishing real wage levels, downsizing, and contingent work have heavily impacted the fate of cities. Cities, after all, have borne the brunt of manufacturing plant closings, have lost vital tax revenue and affluent residents—usually affluent white residents—and have had to deal with growing numbers of people—usually minority residents—whose income and livelihood has worsened. As of 1996, around 16 million city dwellers were caught in the poverty trap. That's a lot of people, about 20 percent of the nation's urban population, double the rate for the suburbs. The smokestack industries, located on the East Coast and in the Rust Belt towns, suffered first, back in the late 1970s and 1980s.

Later, as the 1990s unfolded, mass layoffs also hit places like California, the Northeast, and other parts of the Sun Belt; and these started to affect white-collar workers as well. In California, one in three aerospace workers are now deemed too expensive—"uneconomically viable," as the Michael Douglas character put it in the movie *Falling Down*. There, 234,000 aerospace and specialist high-tech jobs have disappeared since 1988. In Torrance and Long Beach, near Los Angeles, "For Sale" signs blight the landscape; skilled middle-aged men know the daytime TV schedule by heart.[28] These men, like other displaced and deskilled manufacturing workers, like other stagnant relative surplus populations, must try to find jobs in the service sector: maybe, if they're lucky, in maintenance and custodial work, or driving a cab, working the broiler, waiting tables, or cleaning offices.

If jobs haven't already been "outsourced" to the Third World somewhere, then they have probably fled to the newly emerging suburbs and edge cities, where many formerly unionized office and manufacturing industries have sought lower-waged, nonunionized tranquillity. In the process, municipal budgets have been stretched even more and now must face the heat. Consequently, lean production and downsizing doesn't just affect the corporate sector, it gets played out in every nook and cranny of daily life, and is dramatizing a relatively new urban condition: *lean urbanization*. More than anything else, lean urbanization is a city actively downsized, a city whose status assumes the status of a business enterprise. It's a city measured typically by its ability to balance its budget, to operate efficiently, and to maximize its service provision—to maximize at minimal cost.

To be sure, minimizing costs is the hallmark of lean urbanization as it is for lean production. Here municipal councils forever mimic corporate boardrooms. Like their corporate counterparts, city governments all over America have pursued aggressive outsourcing strategies for themselves. Estimates suggest that between 1987 and 1995 the numbers of municipalities contracting-out has increased significantly: janitorial services from 52 percent to 70 percent; street maintenance from 19 percent to 38 percent; waste collection, 30 percent to 50 percent; data processing, 16 percent to 31 percent.[29] Municipalities have pursued competitive bidding for other contracts as well, like construction work and parking lot supervision, and for security and custodial services. Significant cost savings have apparently resulted, mainly from lower overheads, especially lower labor overheads, as specialist service firms tender contracts favorable to finite city council budgets yet unfavorable to the underpaid, overworked labor force. Here, as always, Wall Street and investment rating agencies, like Moody's, look on keenly, eyeing a particular city's business friendliness, assessing its ability to borrow, to raise money and keep taxes low, totting up its financial liability and viability.

In California, then-governor, Pete Wilson, renowned for his anti-union credentials, once schemed to contract-out 50 percent of the state's public sector. "But whether it occurs at the city, county, state, or federal level," says a California Labor Federation spokesman, "privatization usually means a decline in the quality of service, a direct attack on union jobs and wages, and minimal cost savings." (In Buffalo, in 1992, a cleaning contract was negotiated for the state buildings. While claiming that the low contractor offer was based upon efficiency improvements, state officials soon admitted in the *Buffalo News* that savings came about because of "more part-time workers at lower salaries and with fewer benefits.") Thus, there's no evidence that public service delivery necessarily improves through privatization. If anything, the reverse is more likely, given that worker morale is low, absenteeism and turnover is high, and job satisfaction is zilch. So the public sector and city government effectively solicits poverty wage employers and has actively capitalized from them. Cost reductions and trimming of city governments' wage bills effectively ensures the transfer of money from wage earners to employers, to financiers and real estate interests (to FIRE concerns). The transfer comes about in the shape of public subsidy, and businesses have now become the ever-willing recipients of alms designed to absorb market risk.

Corporate welfare is thereby given a distinctively urban bent. It's perhaps a more insidious redistribution of public money than "trickle-down" Reaganomics. Now municipalities—lean cities—accomplish the relatively smooth redirection of revenue into the reconstruction and production of the urban built environment—the all-too-familiar material landscape of office blocks, shopping malls, marinas, and other waterfront development, to say nothing about upscale housing and various sports stadiums. Cost savings made from living labor get capitalized in fixed form, literally in space. These become new geographical configurations wrought by globalization, as well as the context of contemporary U.S. urbanization and the rationale behind a lot of living wage activism; they also give scope to sustained globalization, becoming its veritable platform and material basis.

FIXED CAPITAL: THE LIMITS
OF THE ENTREPRENEURIAL CITY

The capitalization of the urban built environment bears an uncanny resemblance to David Harvey's thesis on the secondary circuit of capital. Investment in the fixed and immobile infrastructure, says Harvey, derives from a redirection, or "switching" of surpluses piled up in the productive primary circuit of capital. As the latter hits crisis and reaches loggerheads in profitability, different fractions of capital can rekindle accumulation by putting idle capital to work into the secondary built environment circuit. Indeed, writes Harvey with a certain persuasion, "analysis of fixed capital formation. . . . in the context of accumulation suggests that investment in the built environment is likely to proceed according to a certain logic." Overaccumulation, he continues, "can be siphoned off—via financial and state institutions and the creation of fictitious capital within the credit system—and put to work to make up the slack in investment in the built environment. The switch from the primary to the secondary circuit may occur in the course of a crisis or be accomplished relatively smoothly depending upon the efficiency of the mediating [and subsidizing] institutions."[30]

Such a practice appears to have happened in many U.S. cities after a lull in the late '80s and early '90s. And it seems equally to occur not necessarily through crisis in the primary circuit but in a diminution of labor power there, enabling capital to benefit in both circuits at once, maintaining profitability on each flank, filching surplus value in production and valorizing it in the production of urban space.

And yet, there are possibilities here—not just threats—for organized labor and place-based people; these circumstances actually reveal that the hypermobility of capital is sometimes overstated. Capital often needs fixity: it isn't always eternally mobile over space, nor can it flit about just anywhere. In certain cases, quite the reverse: tourism, for example, is one industry that can't relocate at whim. Its business is fixed in place, its capital is literally sunk in a specific environment and location, and accumulation hinges on labor power coming together with such fixed capital in that place, nowhere else, certainly not the suburbs, which are hardly on the tourist trail anyway. This place-dependency makes different factions of tourist capital in cities a perfect target for concerted good labor climate offensives. A great deal of HERE Local 11's efficacy in its organizing drives and campaigns in L.A. stems directly from this vulnerability. It's a crucial Achilles' heel in this supposed age of footloose capital: organized labor needs to identify those firms with limited mobility and then hit them hard.

This was vividly borne out in May 2001, when Santa Monica City Council passed one of the nation's most extensive living wage laws. Effective July 2002, it requires those businesses with annual revenues of

$5 million or more in the city's coastal and downtown tourism areas to pay workers at least $10.50 per hour. This is a fair bit over California's current hourly minimum of $6.75. Advocates in Santa Monica claimed that the tourist trade had long benefited from public improvement and subsidy but had failed to share this jackpot with low-rung service workers. "This is the first ordinance that covers a zone that has nothing to do directly with city property or money," beamed LAANE executive director Madeline Janis-Aparicio. "It's one of the biggest victories the living wage movement has ever had."[31] Many businesses and commercial enterprises have highly place-specific requirements and vulnerabilities, as Santa Monica's living wage campaign illustrated, and invariably they need cities. Cities have certain "natural" advantages and possess agglomerations of activities and bundles of ingredients that make them special "relative locations" for capital accumulation. As Pollin and Luce emphasize, "Government subsidies are not usually the primary consideration when businesses make location decisions, though firms push for and happily accept subsidies when offered them."[32]

Those people who can appropriate urban places—like owners of commercial land and buildings—generate appeal to prospective tenants partly because of the facilities and internal configuration of their particular space. Yet many of these ingredients emanate from a much more crucial resource: relative location. The economies of cities are frequently conditioned by relative location. And being fixed in the "right" relative location necessitates a certain commitment to that space, to an urban place, especially for those who wish to garner rent or profit from the enhanced land values of their monopoly situation. Hence, once again, hypermobility of different factions of commercial and landed capital is exaggerated, and shifting about in space isn't a mere frivolous preoccupation. It's not that easy to do. The JfJ campaign recognized this feature well and did their homework on the different players in the building industry, employing full-time researchers to "'ferret out the weaknesses of the ownership/management structure in any particular place."[33] And once the JfJ campaign spread nationwide, there weren't many other places left to run to.

Cutting off exit routes in different cities and in other parts of the same city means somehow translating labor and community struggles over space into action. That's where organizations like LAANE and living wage coalitions come into their own. They can coordinate wider campaigns, reach out from the workplace to the community, build allies, draw in progressive citizens, and centralize their actions while increasingly militant local unions, as affiliates of a larger umbrella group, simultaneously decentralize and democratize the rank and file. Part of L.A.'s labor success derives directly from this double-edged nature of attack: from the ability to fight on two fronts, generalizing a particular campaign, and particularizing the general struggle. The language of class has been their lingua franca throughout. And that's presumably why they've put the fear of God into the city's establishment powers that be. As such, living wage campaigns bear many of the normative hallmarks of the "social-movement unionism" that Kim Moody upholds. "In social-movement unionism," Moody says, "neither the unions nor their members are passive in any sense. Unions take an active lead in the streets, as well as in politics. They ally with other social movements, but provide a class vision and content that make for a stronger glue than that which usually holds electoral or temporary coalitions together."[34]

FIGHT AND FLIGHT

Cities continue to pass living wage ordinances, and still more are being catapulted into debate as grassroots groups turn up the organizing heat. In Milwaukee in 1995 a group called Progressive Milwaukee, allied with the New Party, led the way in a national living wage campaign, winning first a citywide and then a county-wide ordinance. Legislation set a $6.26 hourly wage floor—indexed for inflation—for janitors, unarmed security guards, and parking lot attendants. In 1996, the school board also approved a measure requiring all Milwaukee school system employees to be paid at least $7.70 per hour. "This is a victory for workers and the community," says SEIU's Richard Berghofer. "It's a real first step toward getting people out of poverty." In 1996, Jersey City too passed living wage legislation. There, businesses contracting with the city for clerical, food, janitorial, and security services must now fork over a $7.50 hourly minimum wage; Portland, Oregon, enacted a similar living wage ordinance with $6.25 for fiscal year 1996/1997, $7 for the next fiscal year. In 1997, so did Duluth, Minnesota, $6.50 plus health benefits or $7.25 without; close by, the Twin Cities New Party and ACORN helped Minneapolis–St.Paul follow suit, necessitating all

companies receiving $100,000 or more in public subsidy pay their
workers $8.25 per hour. (St. Paul's JOBS NOW Coalition found that
about 60 percent of newly created private sector jobs in Minnesota in
1993 paid below the livable wage floor.) And San Jose and Boston have
recently waged salutary campaigns.

Still—and perhaps not too surprisingly—in Boston, as elsewhere, the
chamber of commerce and various business interests have vigorously
opposed living wage measures. The Municipal Research Bureau of
Boston contended that legislation may have unintended economic consequences, hindering the creation of new jobs. Thus, a Boston real estate
developer, Robert Beal, immediately announced that a coalition of oppo-
nents will work at repealing the law; they might, he added, even sue the
city. "Business leaders will be discussing this," Beal maintained. "There's
enormous concern out there."[35]

Living wage law, it seems, sends out a bad signal; it suggests a hos-
tile business climate, one that compels capital flight and which thereby puts struggling cities, those ever-eager for capital investment, at a
grave competitive disadvantage. In Minnesota, we've heard this familiar refrain. Their Retail Merchants Association maintained that "man-
dating wages like this will have a chilling effect on business
development"; in Denver, one councilman called their ballot potential
"retail suicide." "What we're going to do," he asserted, "is watch a lot of
our economic base walk out of the city to the suburbs." And over in
L.A., the *Los Angeles Business Journal* thought their living wage legislation
would "derail the economic revival that the City of L.A. has been enjoy-
ing." Such proclamations inevitably find a sympathetic audience. The
local press and mainstream media—those often in cahoots with big
business—are apt to reinforce this *ideological* assault on labor and on
low-wage communities. After all, they control the airwaves and the column space and they can prey off people's hometown loyalty and pride.
Ordinances, the media has it, create the *perception* of a city unfriendly
to business, a city somehow anti-growth, a city that willingly cuts jobs
and is irresponsible about its own future.

Some progressives have responded on the defensive. They've taken on
capitalists at the numbers game, ready to convert vital human experience into remote quantitative spreadsheets or cost-benefit indices. Some
left commentators have tried to emphasize that companies can actually
afford to pay their workers more, and that this won't mean businesses

will lose money, nor will it scare off investors or reduce competitive bidding or lead to eventual job loss. They've defended their camps with diligent and comprehensive reports and monographs, and they've spelled out to the rich and powerful—sometimes in black and white terms, sometimes in italics—that living wages are affordable, that "living wage requirements would be *less than 1 percent of these firms' total costs to produce goods and services.*"[36]

All the while the U.S. working class knows full well that the corporate sector can afford to pay a decent wage. Maybe the crucial point here for progressives isn't defensive economics at all, but offensive *politics*—getting an effective campaign going, being confrontational, getting workers and communities organized, and embracing workers and their allies elsewhere. If there's anything to glean from the L.A. experience, this is surely it. There, activists and unionists have crystallized Marx's insistence that political confrontation and struggles are always ones in which *force* inevitably sanctions the outcome. "The matter," as Marx puts it in *Wages, Price and Profit*, "resolves itself into a question of the respective powers of the combatants." It's only through organizing and campaigning and struggle—individual and collective struggle— that people will discover who they are, how much they're really worth, and how much they can take back: Businesses will never ever give anything up without being forced to. For far too long cities have pivoted upon the urbanization of capital, upon lean urbanization. It's time to struggle for something else, for something more just, for something that's more about the urbanization of labor. In L.A. and elsewhere, it seems that this time may be upon us.

5

Disorder and Zero Tolerance: The Dialectics of Dystopia

THAT CITY WITH ITS SIDE BATHED BY THE SAVIO,

JUST AS IT LIES BETWEEN THE PLAIN

AND MOUNTAIN, LIVES SOMEWHERE BETWEEN

TYRANNY AND FREEDOM.

—Dante, *Inferno*

Dante, writing in the early years of the fourteenth century, refers to a real city, Cesena. The great Italian poet had a keen eye for its peculiar ambivalence. Cesena, he says, lives *somewhere* between tyranny and freedom. Being Dante, that somewhere always seemed to be on the edge of a deep and dark abyss. Even his beloved Florence—especially his beloved Florence—Dante's hometown, which banished him forever, was portrayed in much the same light: "Rejoice, O Florence," he proclaims, "since you are so great, / Beating your wings on land and sea, / That in Hell too your name is spread about!"[1]

With lines like these, Dante sets the tone for some of the liveliest urban realism and criticism in our own day. His portrait of hell, of course, we now recognize as none other than the secular modern city.

These days, many commentaries have intoned how modern cities such as New York, London, and Los Angeles express the best and worst human civilization has to offer. In these cities, the literature says, we find joy and hope fighting it out with nihilism and despair. In these places, the "disconsolate and mutilated shades" that Dante spoke about now transpire as intense poverty, homelessness, and violent crime; and this coexists with enormous personal freedom and mobility, with dazzling stores stocked with every delight under the sun, with movie houses, theaters, restaurants, and nightclubs that suit every taste and fantasy.

But there's another sense in which Dante's urban visions are way ahead of their time: he was, for example, a precursor of an emergent species of writer, a species I shall call *dystopian urbanists*. Dystopian urbanists play around with the received meanings of pain and pleasure in the city. They emerge from different disciplinary backgrounds and hold differing political stances. Many are on the Left. Still more don't recognize the paradoxes of their own analyses and wouldn't admit to their dystopian credentials. And yet all, one way or another, graphically illustrate that there's a perverse allure to urban hell. The ugly, the dangerous, the garish in city life is sometimes a source of attraction; sometimes it's even an impetus for radical politics; occasionally it dramatizes the city itself, simultaneously thrills and appalls, even while you sometimes hate yourself for being thrilled. Try as Mike Davis might to indict twentieth-century Los Angeles in *City of Quartz,* the more he recounts its litany of horrors, the more we want to go there, and the more we, like Davis himself, are mesmerized and fascinated by its dynamics, by its perversity and absurdity.[2]

Similar things can be said about other leftist chroniclers. Take Ed Soja, Fredric Jameson, and Michael Sorkin. As they indict capitalist cities and powerful politicians and planners and the rich and "the logic of capital" their prose soars. But, at the same time, you can't help but hear more than a whisper of admiration and celebration.[3] They each secretly love their city, and why shouldn't they? It's perhaps this value most of all that animates their books and which makes them, like Davis, like urban Marxists everywhere, torn critics. This love of cities and urban life places considerable demands on them and other progressive urbanists. There's always likely to be two souls dwelling within their breasts. This ambiguity is very apparent in one of the first and most intelligent twentieth-century dystopian urbanists, Walter Benjamin. The tension between the low and high life of Paris and Berlin and the Marxist conscience that sought to understand and condemn it, is central to Benjamin's best work—*The Arcades Project, One-Way Street,* and *Charles Baudelaire: A Lyric Poet in the Era of High Capitalism.* Nevertheless, the attraction-repulsion dialectic compels all of us on the Left to consider a troublesome question: Why do we feel drawn to things in cities that we hate and are battling to stamp out? Why is it, as Elizabeth Wilson says, that the "wilderness of Jameson's gleaming car wrecks, the city as dystopia, is as romantic a vision as any"?[4] In this chapter, I want to confront this troublesome question by exploring our lurid fascination with the dystopian city in more depth, especially in more philosophical depth. Inevitably, however, this philosophical concern has practical political and policy overtones. I want to stress that the Left's romance with dystopia exposes Arcadian utopian visions— either Right or Left varieties—of a conflict-free city as hopelessly unrealistic, even hopelessly undesirable, and forces progressives to consider what sort of creative urban initiatives it ought to push for.

THE FLIGHT INTO INTENSITY: THE DYSTOPIAN CITY, THE CITY BEYOND GOOD AND EVIL

Since Dante's day, the city has continued to preoccupy countless thinkers, artists and intellectuals of all political stripes. It's probably true to say that the bulk of them have condemned and expressed moral repugnance toward the city. Unsurprisingly, in its capitalist guise the city has especially been the bone of contention for most liberals and leftists. Carl Schorske has suggested that over the last two hundred years three broad evaluations of the city have pervaded European social thought: the city as virtue, the city as vice, and the city beyond good and evil.[5] It was the medieval city that commanded the more virtuous appraisals. For people like Fichte and Schiller (as for Louis Mumford and Murray Bookchin in our own day), the medieval town symbolized democratic and communitarian ideals, and each thinker pined over artisanal things past. As industrial capitalism started to deepen and broaden, however, Schorske reckons that the idea of the city of vice took hold of the European liberal imagination. After all, it was in cities where poverty, class injustice, dark satanic mills, and rampant individualism prevailed. Hardly any nineteenth-century socialist said anything nice about the industrial urban scene. Marx and Engels were no different from their contemporaries. Of course, all wasn't entirely lost: the city did have the wherewithal to become ultimately virtuous, yet this was a long-term hope. Meantime, we had to endure the dystopian horror of Mammon and Sodom and Gomorrah.

Engels focused more explicitly on the city than Marx. Engels's classic work, *The Condition of the Working Class in England*, penned in 1844–1845, described what the dynamics of capital accumulation does to working people in cities. Cities bear the brunt of industrialization: they house giant factories; they experience vast concentrations of productive forces; they are the foundations of the division of labor and government, of merciless class distinctions and glaring residential ghettoizations. Engels affirmed the capitalist city historically and existentially, yet condemned it ethically. True, the city offered certain freedoms over its feudal counterpart, and in a sense the urban industrial worker was "free." But their freedom, Engels said, was really that of a "free outlaw."

Almost thirty years later, Engels still held this view. In *The Housing Question* (1872), he famously concluded that without revolution and without the total supersession of the market mechanism, no urban reform could rescue the poor, no housing or social initiative could attack the nub of the problem nor string up the real culprits. Instead, it was just shifted someplace else, to another part of town, usually somewhere more politically expedient for assorted capitalists and ruling elites. Urbanization under capitalism could, by the very logic of its own functioning, only ever produce inequality and impoverishment.

Engels's *Housing Question* mercilessly indicts the "tearful" Proudhonist Mülberger for bewailing "the driving of the workers from hearth and home as though it were a great retrogression instead of being the very first condition of their intellectual emancipation." Thus, Marx and Engels felt that the purgatory of the capitalist city is necessary—It's a progressive evil. It's socially disintegrative and disruptive, but it also helps socialize the productive forces; and it brings the masses together where they'll recognize common grievances, organize and unite, wise up, and eventually rise up. Thus, Marx and Engels affirm bourgeois creative destruction because it might be a transitional stage to something more virtuous, something more permanent, less likely to melt into air, where a "real community" of communist citizens could blossom. Just what that future communist city might look like, they never said, nor could ever say.

Some of Marx and Engels's contemporaries took a different tack. Many thrived on paradox and irony. Several were perhaps even more dialectical than Marx and Engels themselves, especially with respect to their urban evocations. Some, like Baudelaire and Dostoevsky, were poets and novelists. Baudelaire, around the same time as Engels's Manchester study, thought Parisian life "rich in poetic and wonderful subjects." "The marvelous," he says, "envelops and saturates us like an atmosphere; but we fail to see it."[6] Marx saw and felt this atmosphere, and was even part of it for a while, but he trivialized it. Indeed, in 1857, when he was writing his enormous *Grundrisse* text in the British Museum, and commuting from Soho to Bloomsbury, Marx existed on a plane far removed from the streets he traversed. In Paris, though, the very same year, Baudelaire wrote of his hometown: "Swarming anthill city, / city gorged with dreams, / where ghosts by day accost passersby, / where mysteries run in defiled canals / like blood that gushes through a giant's vein."[7]

Baudelaire put his finger on the pulse. He emphasized what is positive about alienation and deracination. There is strange joy and freedom, he says, in despair and urban loneliness. Baudelaire reveals how "roaming in the great desert of men," amid the fleeting and transient and contingent, could be grist to a person's mill. For, paradoxically, losing one's fixed identity means discovering new freedoms and other identities, gaining depth and breadth to one's own character, and in the here and now, not in a distant future; it's really all about the "fleeting pleasure of circumstance."[8] Here Baudelaire unveiled the city of vice: if you look hard enough, he says, there's virtue in that vice. His city is "beyond good and evil," or at least the boundaries between good and evil had now been smudged irrevocably. His city is the city of dreadful delight; he really got inside the whale and loved it. Baudelaire shows how urbanites could and should play with fire and construct their cities under Vesuvius. What is repellent had now become weirdly attractive, even a source of inspiration and poetics. Even T.S. Eliot apparently learned this from Baudelaire: "I think that from Baudelaire I first learned, a precedent for the poetical possibilities, never developed by any poet writing in my own language, of the more sordid aspects of the modern metropolis, of the possibility of fusion between sordid realistic and the phantasmagoric, the possibility of the juxtaposition of the matter-of-fact and the fantastic."[9] Baudelaire knew his muse: the *dystopian city* had arrived, a terrible beauty was born and Baudelaire "opened vistas to the city dweller which neither lamenting archaist nor reforming futurist had yet disclosed."[10]

This vista was as scathing of the Left as it was of the Right. In his prose poem, "Let's Beat Up the Poor!" (*Paris Spleen*, no. 49), a satirical and ironical lampoon, Baudelaire tells of how he had for weeks "shut myself up in my room, and had surrounded myself with books fashionable at that time." These "fashionable books," he says, dealt with "the art of making nations happy, wise, and rich, in twenty-four hours. I had thus digested—swallowed, I mean—all the ramblings of all these managers of public happiness—of those who advise all the poor to become slaves, and those who persuade them that they are all dethroned kings." But this "inordinate indulgence in bad books engenders a proportionate craving for fresh air and refreshments." So out Baudelaire goes, toward a tavern. Upon entering, a decrepit old pauper standing outside "held out his hat, with one of those unforgettable looks that would topple thrones." Acting on impulse and instead of giving the fellow the few pence he expects, Baudelaire pounces, smashes the beggar's teeth, grips his throat, and bounces his head against a wall. (Any homeless person will confirm this as an all-too-familiar occupational hazard.)

And yet, Baudelaire's motive here, as we soon realize, is somewhat different from other would-be assailants. For, to the poet's great delight, the pauper begins to retaliate with "a look of hatred that seemed to me a *good omen*" (original emphasis). Quickly, the fellow had blackened Baudelaire's eyes and knocked out two teeth. And the poem—or really the parable—ends with the debate settled, and, content at having established that the poor are always capable of fighting for their rights, the poet remarks: "Sir, *you are my equal!* Please do me the honor of sharing my purse" (original emphasis). The moral, it seems, is that charity and patronage from either do-good reformers or left radicals is even more devitalizing and debilitating than the social evil it's trying to abolish. In Baudelaire's city of dreadful delight, the *fight* for recognition lights up the dystopian sky. "Scenes of high life and of the thousands of uprooted lives that haunt the underworld of the great city," he writes, with characteristic beauty, "are there to show us that we have only to open our eyes to see and know the heroism of our day."[11]

Meanwhile, in St. Petersburg, Dostoevsky exhibited a similar "intensity" toward the city.[12] For him, as for Baudelaire, the city is "the point of departure" in his "flight into intensity."[13] Dostoevsky craves intensity of experience, craves the darker side of humanity, and finds it in the city's depths, in the shady underworld of Russia's great imperial capital. His favorite haunts were gloomy tenement blocks, poor back alleys, and dingy narrow streets in and around Haymarket Square. There he found all types of psychologically damaged, torn, and twisted individuals: déclassé civil servants, losers, alcoholics, gamblers, loners, and petty criminals. Dostoevsky knew a lot of them, and in some probably observed himself. Neighborhoods like these constitute the lifeblood of his novels, and his most fabled characters are ineluctably drawn there. "Dozens of bums and dodgers of every kind and variety," he recalls in *Crime and Punishment,* "thronged the ground-floor chophouses, the dirty, stinking yards of the houses on [Haymarket] square and most of all the cheap bars. These, together with the side streets in the immediate neighborhood, were Raskolnikov's favorite places whenever he went out for a stroll around town. Here his rags attracted nobody's supercilious attention and one could walk as one pleased without scandalizing anyone."[14] Raskolnikov, we are told, often felt impelled to wander these streets whenever he felt sick—to make himself feel sicker.

Here Dostoevsky presents himself as the supreme exponent of a genre Donald Fanger calls "urban gothic."[15] Dostoevsky conveys the melodramatic intensity and hidden luminosity of the city. It's all there if we know how to look. And Dostoevsky, like Baudelaire, certainly knew how to look. His depictions revel in urban paradox and ambiguity. His characters, like the city itself, "teem with opposite elements." St. Petersburg is hated: it has a bad climate and is expensive to live in; it is the "most abstract and intentional city in the whole world." And yet, one of his protagonists says, "I will not leave Petersburg! I will not leave because. . . . Bah, it doesn't matter in the least whether I leave or stay."[16] Hatred and admiration are galvanized into a sort of *fascination.* In great cities, we find novelty and surprise, disorder, thrill, and erotic and sensual fantasy. That is fascination. Fascination is here, even in the city's minutiae—especially in its minutiae.

CRAVING FOR CONTRAST AND CONTRADICTION: DOSTOEVSKY AND MARX ON SUFFERING

The intensity aesthetic, says Alexis de Jonge, "accounts for the peculiar note of exultation with which he [Dostoevsky] describes the wretched poverty-stricken St. Petersburg subculture."[17] Dostoevsky and his characters are plainly pained by what they see and hear and feel, but they're thrilled by it, lured toward it. Pain and suffering for Dostoevsky are a major source of intensity of experience. If Dostoevsky has a central motif in his writing, it's his insistence that human beings crave suffering, need it badly, take from it perverse pleasure. Suffering, he has one of his characters conclude, makes you feel "more alive."

In his short novel *Notes from Underground*, published in 1864, Dostoevsky introduces his long-suffering "Underground Man," a "paradoxicalist" who reminds us that humans are deeply sensuous and spiritual creatures. We are, he says, endowed with consciousness and have the capacity to suffer, to feel pain, to love, lie, and hate. Some of us actually have more than our normal share of consciousness. In fact, such people, such underground people, possess what Dostoevsky calls "hyperconsciousness," a condition accentuated by residing in big cities. These people are acutely perceptive not only about themselves but also about the society in which they live. Their highly developed consciousness comes about through withdrawal and isolation, producing "intensely developed individuality."[18] Naturally they pay an intolerably high price: great emotional and physical suffering. But, according to Dostoevsky, they revel in it. After all, it's only through suffering—"delight in one's own degradation"—that hyperconscious individuals are able to grasp in any depth their own whims and their *"hysterical cravings for contradictions and contrasts."*[19] These people soon come to know the "intricacies of sensuality" and eventually enjoy their sufferings. For them there's even enjoyment in toothache, and the "beautiful and sublime" can be found in the "nastiest, most unquestionable trash."

For Dostoevsky, these characteristics are, more or less, embedded in the human personality. We are all, in one shape or form, "eccentric" people. Some don't admit it or realize it or are afraid to carry it even halfway. Notwithstanding, it ensures that humans can never be merely logical, coolly intellectual, thinking beings. No amount of common sense or reason or science can determine the desirable or what human beings yearn for. Our "hysterical craving for contradictions and contrasts" militates against rational distinctions between pain and pleasure. Sometimes, Dostoevsky says, we lacerate ourselves even when—especially when?—we know it's harmful to do so. In a way we have to, because suffering is the "sole origin of consciousness." On the other hand, it is also the "greatest misfortune for man." He claims that human beings "will devise destruction and chaos, will devise sufferings of all sorts, and will thereby have their own way." Maybe, the Underground Man asks, human beings "like something besides prosperity? Perhaps we like suffering just as much? Perhaps suffering is just as great an advantage to us as prosperity? Man is sometimes fearfully, passionately in love with suffering and that is a fact."[20]

Suffering means doubt, means negation, and "what would be the good of a Crystal Palace if there could be no doubt about it?" In the Crystal Palace, there would be nothing left "but to bottle up your five sense and plunge into contemplation." The Crystal Palace allusion, the real object of Dostoevsky's scorn, is Nikolai Chernyshevsky's radical utopia, his "roseate vision of heroism."[21] The Crystal Palace forms one of the most radiant passages of Chernyshevsky's serialized novel *What Is To Be Done?*, the first installment of which, drafted in prison, appeared in 1863. The key scene is Vera Pavlovna's fourth dream phase where she imagines human perfectibility. Her ideal was symbolized by a "building, an enormous building, such as are now in but a few capitals. . . . or no, there is not a single one like that now! It stands amid fields and meadows, gardens and woods. . . . There is nothing like it now; no, but there is one that points toward it—the palace which stands on Sydenham Hill. Glass and steel, steel and glass, and that is all. No, that is not all, that is only the shell of the building. . . . But there, inside, there is a real house, an enormous house. It is covered by this crystal and steel building as by a sheath. . . . Life is healthy and quiet here. It preserves freshness."[22]

This is Chernyshevsky's invocation of London's Crystal Palace as a microcosm of a rational, ordered, and conflict-free society where all suffering, want, and toil is banished, and where human reason reigns supreme. Apparently, the Russian socialist visited Joseph Paxton's famous structure, the pinnacle of the World's Fair at Hyde Park in 1851, after it had been shifted to the Sydenham Hill site.[23] Dostoevsky, too, had been there, in 1862, and gasped for breadth at the sight of this incarnation of ultimate truth, but recoiled in horror at the thought of living in it: "You feel that here something has been achieved, that here there is victory and triumph. No matter how independent you might be, for some reason you become terrified. 'Hasn't the ideal in fact been achieved here?' you think. 'Isn't this the ultimate, isn't it in fact the "one fold?" Isn't it in fact necessary to accept this as the truth fulfilled and grow dumb once and for all?'"[24] Evidently, Dostoevsky sees the Crystal Palace, as he does Chernyshevsky's utopia, as a facile attempt to apply reason to solve existential dilemmas. And the sort of society purporting to offer total freedom would, Dostoevsky concludes, really be a society of total slavery.

The Crystal Palace prefigured a society based on "mathematical exactitude," where there's "nothing left to do." Then, one would "be neither able to stick one's tongue out nor thumb one's nose on the sly." What worries Dostoevsky so much isn't whether doing away with disorder and painful conflict and chaos is possible, but whether it is *desirable*. Dostoevsky hopes that people will only like utopian Crystal Palaces "from a distance," invent utopias but not really want to live in them. Living in them means the end of novelty, adventure, and fantasy; everything would become routine, the death knell to the human spirit. All passion would be throttled, and who could possibly accept that? From where, asks Dostoevsky, would intensity of experience, the sole origin of consciousness, then emanate?

Ironically, this concern chimed somewhat with that of the youthful Marx. Marx even framed it in strikingly similar terms in his *Economic and Philosophical Manuscripts*.[25] Marx's point of departure here, much like Dostoevsky's, is that humans are endowed with what he calls "vital powers." Vital powers, Marx says, exist in all of us as "dispositions" and "capacities" and "drives."[26] However, "as a natural, corporeal, sensuous, objective being," he adds, humans are "*suffering,* conditioned, and limited beings." Marx suggests that sensuality give humans *reality*. But to be sensuous and *real* one has to be passionate. Yet, Marx is unequivocal: to be passionate it's firstly necessary to *suffer,* to feel pain" (390). (In the original, "suffer"—*leiden*—is always italicized.)

These words appear in a short unfinished essay called "Critique of Hegel's Dialectic and General Philosophy," tucked away at the end of the final "Third Manuscript." In those pages, Marx attacks the "mystifying" speculative philosophy of Hegel's *Phenomenology of Spirit*. While Marx recognizes the positive elements of Hegel, he cannot advocate the priority Hegel conferred to pure, abstract thought. Humans, from Hegel's standpoint, only know themselves for themselves through a reflective self-consciousness. Hegel knew only one kind of labor; Marx calls it "abstract mental labor" and views it as heady "one-sided" stuff. To Marx, it afforded too much credit to thought per se. Hegel implied that consciousness comprised one component, that of knowing as knowing. Perceiving, feeling, suffering, hearing, etc., are all duly downplayed.

Marx holds that humans are "directly natural beings" with their "feet firmly planted on the solid earth and breathing all the powers of nature" (389). Humans know themselves not by turning inward contemplatively, but by reaching out and feeling and seeing and comprehending the external world around them, a world that is simultaneously their own and which incorporates other people. Marx considers the question to be at once ontological and epistemological. As natural beings, he believes, people "must confirm and realize themselves both in their being and their knowing" (391). Still, to have being, one must be sensuous. Sensuality, moreover, is "to be an object of sense, a *sensuous* object, and thus to have sensuous objects outside oneself, objects of one's sense perception. To be sensuous is to *suffer* (to be subjected to the actions of another)" (390). Marx implies that it's precisely suffering which makes us *passionate* beings, and passion is a person's "essential power vigorously striving to attain its object" (390). In short, suffering and passion are some kind of "integral human essence." They are what Marx calls "human effectiveness"; suffering thereby becomes "*an enjoyment of the self for man*" (351) (emphasis added).

Marx wrote the *Manuscripts* to affirm the primacy of "free conscious activity" in the "species-character of man."[27] Here, again like Dostoevsky's *Notes*, he wants to emphasize the importance of free will and individuality. This is why Marx indicts capitalism so ardently, so persistently: it restricts the parameter for free individual development. It is bourgeois society that often treats humans as machines and forces people to behave like "piano keys" and "organ stops," to use Dostoevsky's terminology. To that extent, Marx yearns for a society where people can fully express their individualities and unrealized desires. He wants all the human senses—seeing, hearing, smelling, tasting, feeling, thinking, contemplating, sensing, wanting, acting, loving (these are all Marx's words)—to blossom as "organs of individuality" and "theoreticians in their immediate praxis." Put differently, Marx yearns for a society that intensifies feeling and experience, not one that desensitizes feeling and experience. And this intensification of our capacity to feel and experience would presumably intensify negative as well as positive emotions.

Marx is trying to give suffering a much more positive bent. He's invoking the need for a social and physical environment in which the possibilities for adventure and intrigue would intensify, and so, too, the stimulation of our passions and desires. Maybe that's why he says, so intriguingly, that suffering is "enjoyment of the self for man." Marx is telling us that feeling and suffering—both physical and emotional— is a kind of knowledge. When we feel and suffer we're able to learn things about ourselves that intellect alone can't discern. It's a learning process that, he suggests, is an "integral human essence": it happens to everybody, everywhere, and at all times, whether we like it or not, or whether we confront it or not. Strangely, we need it somehow. Painful and dangerous encounters offer an intensity of experience that equips us to be *whole* people; paradoxically, too, it may even make us *feel* more alive, and helps us stave off what Marx called "one-sided individuality." All told, we, as human beings, crave a society where both positive and negative passions can be played out, openly and honestly. Only then does Marx believe that people might freely and vigorously strive to attain their object. Thus, in the end, despite their metaphysical and political differences, Marx and Dostoevsky become existential bedfellows: both challenge us to imagine more free and open-ended societies.

THE FLIGHT AWAY FROM INTENSITY: HOME REMEDIES AND BIG PLANS

What light does this perspective shed on the dynamics of the city? Maybe it's on the city's shadows and inner recesses where they shine brightest. Both Dostoevsky and the young Marx would insist on the life-enhancing qualities of shadows, of the darker side of existence, where passions and desires and contradictions reside, get acted out, collide, often threateningly, always precariously. Didn't Marx suggest that the senses are "organs of individuality"? Didn't the Underground Man yearn for contradictions and contrasts? Yet didn't he also remind us that this yearning sometimes brought the "greatest misfortune" for human beings?

It's interesting to bring this dialectical analysis into confrontation with perhaps two of the most influential twentieth-century commentators on the city, Jane Jacobs and Lewis Mumford. It's interesting in the sense that the whole question of contradiction and contrast in the city, of disorder versus order, of dystopia versus utopia, animates and gets reenacted in their best-known work. I want to suggest that neither Jacobs nor Mumford got it quite right. I think that Dostoevsky and Marx can give us hints why. Nevertheless, all four can lead us into the contradictions and contrasts of our own urban scene, and pinpoint the sorts of questions we now urgently need to ask.

Jane Jacobs starts off in a vein reminiscent of Dostoevsky. She's dead against big ideals and radiant visions. For her, the city isn't a work of art nor is it a "garden" or anything "beautiful" in the sense that planners conceive it. Instead, she maintains that true descriptions of urban reality are "drawn not from how it ought to be, but how it is." And when you look at how it is, Jacobs thinks, you find some pretty amazing things going on: "The way to get at what goes on in the seemingly mysterious and perverse behavior of cities is, I think, to look closely, and with as little previous expectation as possible, at the most ordinary scenes and events, and attempt to see what they mean." Surprisingly, Jacobs says, "most of the material lies at my own front door." Soon she opened her front door, stepped outside, looked around at her Greenwich Village neighborhood, inspecting its streets, its people and children, its shops and bars and parks. Then, in 1961, her findings were published in a now canonical text, *The Death and Life of Great American Cities: The Failure of Town Planning*.[28]

Jacobs lambastes Ebenezer Howard and the whole Garden City movement. "His aim," she observes, "was the creation of self-sufficient small towns, really very nice towns if you were docile and had no plans of your own and did not mind spending your life among others with no plans of their own" (27). For her, however, cities worked best when they deliberately encourage spontaneous diversity and teemed with all sorts of activity and behavior. The commingling of multiple functions, services, shops, and people in the same block brought life to neighborhoods and helped cities flourish—both socially and economically. Jacobs defends disorder and messiness, and says the differing degrees of social contact and continual neighborhood activity creates "intricate street ballets," which "eddy back and forth" day and night. And because these streets are animated, they attract more people, all kinds of people, who want to wander and loiter and live in its environs. Meanwhile, dynamic sidewalk life bolsters safety: "A well-used street is apt to be a safe street."

Jacobs highlights that there's beauty and an abundance of life in the ostensibly disordered street. Its day-to-day functioning is a subtle and highly developed organism that needs watering and nurturing, not wholesale bulldozing and rebuilding anew. Ordered, homogeneous neighborhoods need staving off. Planners hedge people's craving for contrast and contradiction and socially engineer sterile spaces, believing them beneficent for humanity. Planners, says Jacobs, have little real idea about the pleasures of urbanity or about what makes cities tick. Their prescriptions to save the city from its raving pathologies of congestion and overcrowding—by reducing numbers to "normal" proportions and through stiff zoning regulations—only "do the city in."

Lewis Mumford, conversely, considered this line "comical in its inaccuracy" and vented his rancor at Jacobs's "home remedies."[29] He used his influence at the prestigious *New Yorker* magazine to defend planning with "hate in his heart."[30] To begin with, he concurred with Jacobs: a neighborhood "is not just a collection of buildings but a tissue of social relations and a cluster of warm personal sentiments, associated with the familiar faces of doctor and priest, the butcher, the baker and the candlestick maker, not least with the idea of 'home.'" True, too, this "able woman had used her eyes and, even more admirably, her heart to assay the human result of large-scale housing. . . . [and] saw more deeply into the plight of both those who were evicted and those who came back to live in homogenized and sterile barracks that had been conceived in terms of bureaucratic regimentation, financial finagling, and administrative convenience." But from a gallant "sense and sensibility" there emerges, Mumford thinks, a "pride and prejudice."

Underneath her thesis, which suggests that the sidewalk, the street, and the neighborhood in all their "higgledy-piggledy unplanned casualness" are the very heart of urban vitality, Mumford argues, lies "a preoccupation that is almost an obsession: the prevention of criminal violence in big cities." He accuses Jacobs of having an "overruling fear of living in the big city she so openly adores, and, as all New Yorkers know, she has considerable reason for fear." Yet her belief that planners shouldn't interfere, and that everything should be kept small-scale and intimate, that shops and houses and people should be mixed together, is, he thinks, absurd for ameliorating criminal violence and urban malaise. If that's really the case, Mumford says, "eighteenth-century London, which met all of Mrs. Jacobs's planning prescriptions, would not have been the nest of violence and delinquency it actually was." For Mumford, the problem of cities is more fundamental and deep-rooted: "overgrowth, its purposeless materialism, its congestion, and its insensate disorder—the very conditions she vehemently upholds as marks of vitality."

Even things that Jacobs deals with best—like face-to-face interactions on the street, the common interest of certain neighborhoods, the stability of family relationships—rest not on metropolitan dynamism but, Mumford maintains, on "continuity and stability" and on "the special virtues of the village." Her urban vision, in other words, is a pastoral vision. It is a vision that is almost folksy and conservative in its defense of neighborhood integrity in the face of metropolitan expansion. Therein resides an irreconcilable tension in the Jacobs argument: a destructive antagonism between her pursuit for neighborhood life, on the one hand, and her "unqualified adoration of metropolitan bigness and dynamism," on the other. Mumford suggests that this tension can be reconciled by the institution of planning and urban design.

To this extent, he seeks to address market growth and penetration; he believes that market forces annihilate neighborhood intimacy in the long run. His response follows the shibboleths of Howard's Garden City model and Geddesian reformism, arguing that there are "natural limits" to capitalist urban growth. So Mumford's city is an organism that has its limits and if it expands beyond those limits it cannot sustain itself as a healthy life-form. At such a point, the humanist planner enters the fray to perform the necessary radical surgery. It is the planner who orchestrates decentralization, who breaks the city down into a series of smaller manageable units. From this standpoint, Mumford's city is a vast work of art, and it is the task of the great artist-planner to create a dignified and democratic expression of human culture. His urban vision is obviously romantic. Specifically, it romanticizes the past: the Greek city, Mumford wrote in *The City in History*, was "neither too small nor too big, neither too rich nor too poor, it kept the human personality from being dwarfed by its own collective products."[31] He equally reminisces about the medieval town, his urban ideal. He shares this nostalgia with his great antagonist.

So, although Mumford and Jacobs approach the urban question from different scales and from different standpoints, they each end up with not so much an antiurban manifesto as an *antimetropolitan* one. Mumford, though, probably goes further with his antimetropolitan bias. He, remember, fled New York City for his cherished Amenia, a small upstate New York town, where he spent most of his adult life. It was he who hated the New York skyline, reviled skyscrapers and the city's bustle and congestion, noise and blight. Mumford got out of New York City at the same time many other people wanted to move in, and for those very same reasons Mumford wanted out. The humble virtues Mumford yearned for—harmony, moderation, poise, symmetry, organic balance—are worlds removed from what a lot of city dwellers sought or still seek, and from the sort of metaphysics that Dostoevsky and Marx affirm.

Of course, Mumford is no dystopian. He's an urbanist of the old school. His prescriptions lurch toward pragmatic utopianism. He claims to be a big-city boy, but he clearly has small-town values. His notion that disorder is somehow antihuman and antiorganic reveals these small-town values. Nor is disorder somehow insensate. The young Marx and Dostoevsky would beg to differ: it is disorder, they say, that enables the senses to become "theoreticians in their immediate praxis." It is disorder that enables us to feel more, and provide us with "enjoyment of the self." Mumford even appears to agree with the greatest champion of order, Plato, who in Book Ten of *The Republic* says, "If you receive the pleasure-seasoned Muse of song and epic, pleasure and pain will be kings in your city instead of law." Jacobs grasps the uses and pleasures of disorder much better than her longtime adversary.[32] She's maybe only a short step away from emphasizing the allure of dystopia itself. But she can't quite bring herself around to make that step. Her focus on safety and villagey intimacy wrenches her away in the other direction. In the end, both Mumford and Jacobs seem to shy away from the flight into intensity that Marx and Dostoesvky endorse.

Forty years later, Mumford and Jacobs's urban visions sound somehow defensive and prudish. For one thing, neither ever imagined how disorder and danger, even ecological disruption, might be *enticing* as well as unnerving. And it's enticing precisely *because* it's unnerving. Neither considered that this, too, is what gives the city its problematical energy. Nor did they realize that those self-same destructive forces are linked to things we crave for and seem unwilling to give up at any cost, and in the city we invariably find them: mobility, novelty, abundance, and freedom from traditional virtues and pieties. Modern tragedy, Alfred Kazin aptly says, "is unreflectiveness, apartness in our hearts from the lives we actually live and drive others to live."[33] Neither Jacobs nor Mumford thus ponder the tragic joy of dystopia. Neither recognized how, somehow, we are liberated by dystopia. Needless to say, it's a liberation we pay dearly for. It is, of course, our very own Faustian pact with the devil. But in that pact we can sometimes discover ourselves as persons.

Neither Jacobs nor Mumford understood the social and psychological dynamics of the *unsustainable city*. The unsustainable city is always the dystopian city, always a city on the edge, on the edge of a social and ecological precipice. But it is *alive* on that edge, not stable or moribund or safe. That it has an edge is surely its whole reason for existence anyway. Of course, it puts people on edge and sometimes tips you over the edge. And yet, a lot of people crave that edge. While many people, particularly middle-class people, have fled cities over the last couple of decades for the relative security and cost-effectiveness of the suburbs, others—often young, single people—have gone to cities to escape community and stability and continuity. They go to cities to invent and reinvent themselves. Some, if they can commandeer sufficient economic resources, succeed. Many more love cities because they can be rootless. As the other Marx, Groucho, quipped, "Home is unquestionably where the heart is, but it is also the place where you bathe, change your clothes, and get the hell out of as quickly as possible." Sometimes, people yearn actively *not to belong*. Many follow the sentiments of Baudelaire or Dostoevsky's Underground Man, even if, as is likely, they don't ever know it. This sense of "breakdown"—be it familial or moral or both—isn't a symptom of disruption or anarchy but a symptom of progression and freedom, and of life. The transcendence of "basic" values, especially those that place people in roles or boxes or force them to operate under moral taboos or temporal and spatial prohibitions, is to be celebrated not denounced.

FROM THE USES OF DISORDER TO "ZERO TOLERANCE"

Unfortunately, many of today's politicians and ruling classes, both sides of the Atlantic, fully understand the dynamics of disorder and want to suppress it. None of which is to say that there aren't problems with certain forms of disorder. Nor is the unsustainable city a city that prostrates itself before a rampant corporate capitalism. But the added dilemma is that those who want to suppress disorder aren't exclusively on the Right now. Intolerance of urban disorder has been voiced on the British center Left, too, and it has caused considerable political furor. Speaking loudest was Labour Home Secretary Jack Straw, whose views were publicly endorsed by boss Tony Blair.

Straw was influenced by a 1995 report called "The Year of Change: Re-engineering the New York City Police Department," the brainchild of former New York mayor Rudy Giuliani and ex-police chief William Bratton. Their report inaugurated a now-familiar term and tactic for dealing with street convulsions and disorder in the Big Apple: zero tolerance. This get-tough policy on vagrancy, panhandling, squeegee men, petty criminality, and graffiti tries to stamp out public misdemeanor, however minor, by employing an intensified police presence. It purports to tackle relatively minor disorders before they can escalate into more serious crime—the so-called broken windows thesis. The goal is nothing other than "civic cleanliness." Indeed, zero tolerance in New York boasts resounding successes: crime rates have fallen 40 percent over recent years; the city's annual murder total has dropped below the 500 mark, which is more than half the figure for 1990. Although many criminologists warn that other factors are responsible here—like the changes in New York's economic fortunes, the relative decline of numbers of teenage males in the nation's population, stabilizing turf and gang wars[34]—zero tolerance initiatives have nonetheless impressed Labour government bigwigs. London's notorious King's Cross—long a gruesome site of crack dealing, drug abuse, prostitution and vagrancy—has been a test case, and a six-week-long experiment there deployed extra "high-profile" police foot patrols.

Zero tolerance, not surprisingly, is controversial. Liberals have been up in arms about the potential threat to civil liberties.[35] The biggest complainants are the homeless, who now get moved on with no place else to go. Many exist on the street, even have a rightful place on the street, are somehow *of* the street, however problematical this might be for them and for everybody else passing by. With zero tolerance, one can't help wonder whether the baby of disorder might be getting ditched with the criminal bathwater. While it's evident that disorder can lead to crime, it's also evident that not all disorder is criminal. The strategy also exhibits a *denial* of what the city is.[36] Jane Jacobs herself wanted disorder, but she also appealed for safety and neighborhood, for face-to-face intimacy. Intimacy, in turn, implies some sense of inwardness and cohesiveness; and neighborhood inwardness and cohesiveness matched with the desire for safety might beget some pretty repressive implications—like zero tolerance. Indeed, those who endorse disorder but who fear crime, like Jacobs, better watch out that those who also fear crime but hate disorder don't stamp out the sort of disorder that's so fundamental to a vibrant urban culture. Moreover, a busy street may be a safe street, but if it's a *metropolitan* street it will have lots of people using it, different people, not all of whom will be local or familiar. Busy streets offer individual freedom, anonymity, and scope for invisible behavior, some of which might even be criminal; it's difficult to see a modern metropolitan street as anything otherwise.

In recent years, Jacobs has become a cult heroine for other champions of order. In *Fixing Broken Windows: Restoring Order and Reducing Crime in Our Communities*, the conservative duo George Kelling and Catherine Coles enthusiastically invoke Jacobs.[37] "Order arises," they say, "out of what Jane Jacobs has called the 'small change' of urban life: the day-to-day respect with which we deal with others and the concern that we exercise for their privacy, welfare, and safety."[38] "What is disorder?" Kelling and Coles ask. "In its broadest sense, it is incivility, boorish and threatening behavior that disturbs life, especially urban life." Reading between the lines, we soon discover the real target of Kelling and Coles's antipathy: civil libertarians, especially 1960s radicals, who have pioneered the growth of individualism and individual rights. In short, these radicals, Kelling and Coles say, have "helped spur an increase in deviant behavior on city streets, while changes in legal doctrine, especially in constitutional and criminal law, not only permitted such behavior to continue but safeguarded the rights of those behaving in deviant fashion. Said in another way, disorder grew and was tolerated, if not ignored, because the expression of virtually all forms of nonviolent deviance came to be considered synonymous with the expression of individual, particularly First Amendment or speech-related, rights."[39] Thus, Bruce Shapiro is dead right when he suggests that broken windows and zero tolerance initiatives aren't really "about crime at all, but [are] a vision of social order disintegrating under glassy-eyed liberal neglect."[40] It is, in a nutshell, "an illusory obsession with order at all costs."[41]

Of course, everyday street life—the directly immediate, palpable, and observable world—is the scale for giving meaning and substance to everybody's lives. To feel safe and happy in the street and in urban public space is an existential priority. Nevertheless, the street *internalizes* other forces and other realities—abstract forces and processes, which, as Marx warned us in *Capital,* are sometimes "imperceptible to the senses." Accordingly, it takes a special kind of thinking person to see and feel at once concrete *experience* and abstract *processes* and then try to live them out and understand them as one world, in their totality. (Antonio Gramsci suggested that "organic intellectuals" were equipped with this special kind of sensibility.) True, homelessness, street begging, and alcoholism are conditioned by a whole array of complex psychological, personal, and domestic factors. (Homeless women, for instance, have often fled their homes to escape male domestic violence.) As these factors manifest themselves concretely in daily life, out on the street, they're often seen as pathological, as nuisances that have to be endured and experienced by "ordinary" passersby. And yet, if the personal and individual is taken relationally and embedded in a broader socioeconomic and political context, which both incorporates and conditions individual agency, a different truth bursts forth.

In this sense, the zero-sum trajectory of urban society in terms of housing, jobs, and future hopes—between the haves and have-nots, between the "ins" and the "outs"—unfurls on the street itself for everybody to see, hear, and encounter each day, *but not always understand fully.* City streets in the United States, and increasingly in Britain, bare the grisly scars of a society with ideological and material aversion to public policy, which favors private greed over civic virtue. Thus, in the street, domestic and personal circumstances cascade and become exacerbated by macro and structural contradictions; a relentless and vicious dialectic takes hold, leaving many people teetering on the edge of the abyss, and some plunge into it. Yet dialecticians have a distinctive role to play in revealing these ties, of pointing out subtle links as well as brutal interconnections. and, above all, making them known to the public at large. Dialecticians, in short, have a responsibility to promote further a critical understanding of the world.

For that reason, Gramsci argued that dialectical analysis shouldn't be an abstract "higher" mode of thought, but should enter into *people's common sense itself*—which, we know, contains both truth and misrepresentation. Accordingly, although some people will still feel threatened and intimidated by the convulsions of the street, with a deeper knowledge of the mechanisms *producing* this grim scenario they might at least be able to look street people in the eye and have greater patience and compassionate for them. Meantime, greater knowledge of the *underlying* injustices could spark anger and disgust at a society that either normalizes or criminalizes such circumstances, and seeks to play people off against one another and use all forms of prejudice and intolerance to motivate wealth creation and prosperity. Arguably, then, policing and urban policy shouldn't stifle public disorders and uncertainty, nor should they crush street spontaneity and vibrancy. On the other hand, a democracy cannot allow all types of disorder to run amok. While some of us, as Plato observed, have unconscious desires to commit murder, incest and rape—even though we "have every appearance of being decent people"—not everyone "expresses in waking reality" these impulses. Sharing public space with those who do express it in conscious waking reality might, unsurprisingly, force many people to stay away.

Unpalatable "deviant" people, of course, are more problematical for the Left than the Right. The latter would simply be happy with any solution that gets them out of *their* sight. Differentiating "bad" from "good" disorder necessarily involves negotiation and argument, as well as a toleration of conflict, discordance, and painful encounter, which has always had a rightful place in an authentic urban culture. But disentangling "good" from "bad" disorder mustn't relapse into the kind of logic Dostoevsky's Ivan Karamazov preached, whereby one might love people at a distance or in the abstract but hate them close up, as neighbors, in all their concrete messiness. Making these choices requires something more than zero tolerance. It involves holistic welfare initiatives, a rebuilding of assorted public institutions, a deeper understanding of what gives cities their frightening force and awesome grandeur. The Left has to fend off and contest zero tolerance tactics while it tries to formulate what the *city of tolerance* might look and feel and function like, negotiating the "despotism" of urbanization—whose battle cry is order—and the "anarchy" of urbanism—whose lifeblood is disorder.

Those of us on the Left who yearn for social justice, and also love cities, find ourselves torn between the tyranny we see around us every day and the thrill that same tyrannical city can sometimes offer. How can alternative visions and strategies be devised that can promote the latter while negating the former? Does the just city have to be a sterile one? How are we to whet the appetite of our inextricable craving for contrast and contradiction while staving off painful nihilism? Or, on the other hand, is painful nihilism something we need? If it is, how can we harness it positively, use it as a creative as well as destructive force? This poses both philosophical and practical policy dilemmas, and the time is ripe to consider such dilemmas seriously and unflinchingly. But the theme is always likely to leave leftists in some paradoxical position. We can see such a position infuse Davis's *City of Quartz*: it's that which makes it a book worth reading. We can also think of other instances were the Left is often compelled to give up unsoiled purity, defend sleaze, vice, and violence, and assume awkwardly defensive postures. The recent fate of New York's Times Square illustrates these dilemmas.

BETWEEN UTOPIA AND DYSTOPIA:
THE SPECTACLE OF TIMES SQUARE

This little piece of America is now embroiled in all sorts of finagling involving the city and big capital. The biggest player is Disney, which has set up operations in the New Amsterdam Theater on 42nd Street and bullied the City of New York to spearhead a massive cleanup campaign and commercial redevelopment scheme. Helped along by the 42nd Street Development Corporation and the Times Square Business

Improvement District (BID)—established in 1992 to provide sidewalk, curbside, and anti-graffiti crusades, around-the-clock security patrols, pornography regulation, and other public "improvements"—Disney is playing hardball in cleansing the district. With lots of "sweetheart deals" and "corporate welfare" on offer, endorsed by a glittering array of architectural luminaries—such as Philip Johnson and Robert Stern— retail strips and shopping malls, high-rise offices, TV studios, hotels, and a multiplex cinema continue to mushroom.[42]

Unable to disguise nostalgia for the Golden Age of Times Square, the Left has voiced its disapproval. Christine Boyer, for one, expresses a typical lament, and in a familiar argot: "We have allowed a quintessential public space of an American city to be redesigned as a simulated theme park for commercial entertainment. Architect Robert A. M. Stern's interim refurbishment plan extrapolates from the realism of the area's popular and commercial features and returns this to privileged spectators who can relish the illusion in a sanitized and theatricalized zone."[43] Of course, that quintessential public space has always been one of vivid encounter and entertainment and an illicit sexual marketplace—which is, if you think about it, is a peculiar thing for leftists to defend in the first place. And yet, Times Square since 1905 has been a special kind of open-minded public space, along with all the hazards this engenders. Home of Tin Pan Alley, vaudeville and burlesque and Ziegfeld Follies, risqué and "legitimate" theater, wise guys and dolls, peep and porn shows, drug pushers and hustlers and hipsters, the neon light of the Great White Way has shone brightly and created dark brooding shadows. It has traditionally satisfied an array of urban appetites and fantasies, challenged norms of public morality and behavior—norms about "private parts in public places"[44]—and infused itself into the popular psyche of New Yorkers and Americans alike. It has been a place where fortunes are made and lost, hearts are broken, and dreams become nightmares. No surprise that Times Square has captured the imagination of successive generations of writers, poets, filmmakers, playwrights, and musicians.

But Times Square has been long denounced by moralists. In the past, as now, it was viewed as a "cesspool of filth and obscenity."[45] It was equally, as William Sherman's hard-boiled reportage in *Times Square* illustrates, a popular haven. At the habitual New Year's Eve celebrations, says Sherman, "some of the men at the party had served on the cleanup of Times Square." Formulating their own zero tolerance plans, these people "met in plush offices over coffee and Danish pastries and considered new zoning, new penal codes, anti-prostitution drives, more cops, curfews, padlocks for the porno stores, even closed-circuit TV monitors for the worst blocks, and lawsuits to close the seamiest hotels. But while they partied on the roof, down below at the very crossroads of the world, a mammoth 'pornucopia' featuring the very latest in prepubescent masturbation magazines was open and doing a brisk business—even on New Year's Eve."[46]

Times Square was also a haven for gay hustlers and lonesome exiles. John Rechy was there for a while and in *City of Night* wrote of how he surrendered to its world: "I stand on 42nd Street and Broadway looking at the sign flashing the news from the Times Tower. . . . The world is losing. The hurricane still menaces. . . . I feel explosively excited to be on this street—at the sight of the people and lights, sensing the anarchy. . . . like a possessive lover—or like a powerful drug—it lured me. FASCINATION! I returned, dazzled, to this street. The giant sign winked its welcome: FASCINATION!"[47] This winking fascination now takes on a new twist. New millennium Times Square has driven Rechy's furtive and underground men elsewhere, just like Engels said, and habitués of the square are currently beguiled by a gigantic cylindrical winking sign, the most electronically advanced surface known to humans; the $20 million Nasdaq sign. It gives up-to-the-minute stock prices for one hundred high-tech and Internet companies while projecting two ads a minute. Nearby are billboards as big as buildings, exhibiting graphic spreads of beautiful bodies, FASCINATION, promoting the likes of The Gap, L'Oréal, Liz Claiborne, Tommy Hilfiger, and the hip TV show, *Sex in the City*. At nighttime, this spectacle becomes incandescent, even more seductive and sexy and fascinating, and Times Square's allure beams out farther and farther up Broadway, right out across America.

Today, Times Square isn't just a spectacle: it's perhaps *the* fascinating spectacle; a veritable media orgy, colonized by Disney, Condé Nast, Bertelsmann, Virgin, MTV, Madame Tussaud, Ernst Young, Reuters et al. Lonely underground men have long given way to rich overground executives. Moreover, in and around the "new 42nd Street," sandwiched between Broadway and Eighth Avenue, cranes, scaffolding, and vacant lots betoken further spectacular redevelopment ahead. Herbert

Muschamp, resident architectural correspondent of the *New York Times*, argues that Times Square is the leading exemplar of a "manufactured center." But its most impressive and beguiling architecture, Muschamp admits, isn't actually embodied in bricks and mortar, isn't the new office towers; instead, it's high-tech signs, those huge glowing facades and billboards, icons of our consumerist age. Here surface is everything, depth nothing. Here "thing-commodities" have been supplanted by "image-commodities." Muschamp invokes the late French Situationist theorist Guy Debord as confirmation. In his blurb to the *New York Times Magazine*'s color photo spread, "The Guts of Times Square" (October 22, 2000), Muschamp says Debord was "prophetic": after all, the latter's masterpiece, *The Society of the Spectacle*, anticipated "the conversion of the public into consumers of banal visual experience."

THE POLITICS OF THE SPECTACLE
IN TIMES SQUARE

Thirty-odd years on, banal visual experience is precisely what Times Square revels in. Yet its whole raison d'être straddles the dystopian dialectic, even as it tries to re-create a banal corporate utopia, a Disney Crystal Palace. Debord was one of the twentieth-century's most apt prophets of dystopia. Muschamp plainly considers him right, but nevertheless likes the new Times Square: "Brainwashed American image-shopper that I am, I am a big fan of the new Times Square." He invokes Debord's spectacle, but then makes a spectacle out of Debord. He admires Debord's questioning, postures with Debord's radical critique, but then flees from Debord's real radicalism, backs away from his politics. Debord saw that type and their world coming way back; he would have hated both Muschamp and the new Times Square, would have wanted no part in their show biz, celebrity shallowness. Between 1957 and 1972, Guy Debord was one of the leading lights in a subversive political movement called the Situationists. They were romantic young men and women—avant-garde artists, writers, poets, and students—many of whom became the brains and the brawn of the May 1968 insurrection. Then, for a little while, the city was theirs, "imagination seized power," and a spontaneous freedom erupted on the Paris streets. They hurled Molotov cocktails and threw bricks, ripped up paving stones, searched for the beach and wanted the world. Once the dust settled, and once the wreckage became institutionalized, Debord and his generation spent years wandering around in the night getting consumed by fire.

As the flames raged throughout the conservative 1980s and "Third Way" 1990s, Debord's defiant legacy and the Situationists' restless spirit somehow linger. We can find it in Debord's books, which continue to sell, continue to speak to lots of people, especially to progressive people alienated from ballot box party politics. If anything, the relevance of Debord's message, and the vitality of his radical politics, grows stronger the more his books date. Meanwhile, we can glimpse a reinvigorated, twenty-first-century Situationism out on our very own streets today, engaging in their very own dystopian politics. In fact, the street is where we can really begin to understand the spectacle of Debord. It's there where we can locate his theory *and* his praxis, his hard-nosed Marxism and his free-spirit anarchism. In a nutshell, it's in our own streets where we can still find the Debord that Muschamp doesn't mention. Once we've found him, we can return to Times Square.

At its most fundamental level, *The Society of the Spectacle* warns us of the degree to which the commodity pervades our daily lives. Debord shows how its logistics stoop to new depths as he takes Marx's analysis to new heights. He presents his case for the prosecution idiosyncratically and hyperbolically, in the form of 221 short theses, aphorisms reminiscent of Marx's own on Feuerbach. Yet Debord unites Marx's youthful humanism with his mature political economy, emphasizing the unbroken lineage between alienation and fetishism, between his existentialism and his science, while delving into the belly of the spectacular beast. *The Society of the Spectacle* is really a radical critique and a call to arms. Its theoretical analysis seeks to puncture the fetishism and name the alienation; its war cry stirs the Left to mobilize and organize, summoning up active human agency to confront "spectacular contemplation."

In Thesis #1 of *The Society of the Spectacle*, Debord paraphrases Marx: "In societies where modern conditions of production prevail, all of life presents itself as an immense accumulation of spectacles." He says, "Everything that was directly lived has moved away into a representation." Now, all of us inhabit "a pseudo-world apart," a world where specialized images, global satellite networks, and high-tech gadgetry and multimedia dominate and cohere as "autonomous images." Now, it's a world gone "topsy-turvy," where "the true is a moment of the false." And this falsity, moreover, reigns as "an instrument of unification." Now, we have our twenty-first century lingua franca, a vocabulary everyone knows instinctively: the gospel according to MTV and CNN, to Bill Gates and Rupert Murdoch, to McDonald's big "M" and Nike's phantasmagoric swoosh. Such a world "says nothing more than 'that which appears is good, that which is good appears'" (Thesis #12). Under modern spectacular capitalism, Marx's "estranged labor" generalizes into "estranged life"; a "false consciousness of time," time turned into an abstraction, time abandoned. Thus, for Debord, spectacular time represents an eternal present, the denial of death, a Disney simulation, the real fake. The spectacle marks capitalism's seizure and denigration of history and memory. Its seizure and denigration of time likewise signals its seizure and denigration of space, which becomes an abstract space of the market. City space, especially, becomes commodified, colonized, bought and sold, torn down, speculated on, fought over. Space, like time, must be organized, ordered, and patrolled. Disorderly old streets threaten the spectacular status quo, and "efforts of all established powers to increase the means of maintaining order in the streets finally culminate in the suppression of the street" (Thesis #172).

Debord believed in revolutionary class struggle, but this struggle had to embed itself in daily life and employ different kinds of rambunctious maneuvers to subvert this daily life. Carefully planned organization underwrote disruptive and explosive street spontaneity. This made for a less predictable, more independent, and confrontational left politics. Dionysus and Apollo meet in the street: Marx provides the practical theory, Rabelais a carnival spirit, Clausewitz realpolitik. Now, politics became akin to war, "the domain of danger and disappointment," of "forces in contention and the contradictory necessities imposed on the operations of each of the two parties."[48] A central feature of the Situationists' realpolitik was *détournement*, or "hijacking," which monkey-wrenched accepted bourgeois meaning, behavior and tradition. Squatting, sit-ins, occupations, raucous street demonstrations, as well as graffiti and "free associative" expressionist art are typical examples of *détournement*. Streets become the stage and stake in doing harm to the spectacle; in effect, they become spectacular counter-spectacles, sites of new "situations," spaces where things get turned around, where meaning gets transformed into nonsense, and nonsense into meaning. *Détournement* meant collective feats of resistance—some serious and epic, others playful and absurd. At best, these acts of protest and defiance would become infectious "festivals of the people," recalling the glory days of the 1871 Paris Commune, and enacted on the streets of Paris ninety-seven years later. "To be free in 1968," one wall graffito read then, "is to participate."

If we change some of the hairstyles and fashions of those participating, we might swear that Debord and his Situationist friends were actually on New York's streets, in Times Square, in November 1999. It was the Friday after Thanksgiving, the busiest shopping day of the year, in the middle of the holiday rush, and Times Square was briefly "liberated" by "people power." Unfurling on the street was a mass "Festival of Resistance," a celebration of "Love and Life," orchestrated by a fascinating fledgling (and neo-Situationist) crew called Reclaim the Streets (RTS). In recent years, in many different countries, RTS has grown fast, becoming something of a global protest network for dissatisfied people, for those who still care a lot about the fate of our cities, about democracy, about corporations and supranational institutions taking over the world. They've closed down busy streets in Sydney, Australia, in north, south, and central London, and in countless other European cities. In all these places, crowds have danced, shouted, and partied, men and women (and children) from diverse backgrounds: revolutionaries, students, dancers, workers, activists, madmen, malcontents. They've brought traffic to a standstill, engaged in various pranks and exhibitionist behavior, demanded pedestrians' and bikers' right to the city, and transformed "stretches of asphalt into a place where people can gather without cars, without shopping malls, without permission from the state and develop the seeds of the future in present society."

In New York, to deceive the cops, prior notices suggested Union Square was the site of RTS/NYC protest. When the authorities closed in there, around a small dancing group, the real action erupted in Times Square. It took an hour before New York's finest could break up the rally. As the police moved protesters on, roughing up a few and carrying them off in paddy wagons, on show were the same "zero tolerance" and "quality of life" programs activists had been contesting—initiatives that have cracked down on problematical public spaces, like "old" Times Square, together with their problematical populations. They've helped cleanse and clean up a lot of grubby streets and frayed buildings, shifted a lot of vulnerable people elsewhere, usually out of sight, and reordered an often legitimate disorder. Former public spaces quickly find walls built around them, undergo privatization, and get airbrushed by corporate logo. Elsewhere, spectacular architecture and Business Improvement Districts bring redemption. Whatever route, the city falls to the highest bidder. Some spaces even forbid groups of more than twenty people from congregating, thus muting political activity and narrowing democracy. In fact, Giuliani's disdain for "free speech" is pretty legendary, as is his paranoia about a "Red menace." His quality-of-life program, accordingly, has an explicit political goal, tellingly headlined by the *New York Times*: "Giuliani's New Mission: Get Marxists Off the Streets." "Marxism unfortunately is still alive in parts of New York City, even in the latter part of this century," bemoaned the mayor, "even though it's been disgraced all over the world."[49] A sinister Marxist tinge, he said, can be traced in a variety of enemies, from those sacking Starbucks and McDonald's in Seattle, right under the noses of World Trade Organization (WTO) bigwigs, to placid gardeners who plant flowers and vegetables in New York's numerous community gardens.

Needless to say, Giuliani is right about one thing: Marxism *is* alive and kicking; and its Situationist strand was palpable in Seattle, too. Indeed, in the wake of the Times Square rumble, RTS, alongside other radical umbrella organizations like Global Exchange pioneered "Seattle's Citizen Committee," a driving force in the rowdy demonstrations against the WTO meeting. But the spectacular society, which the WTO and its ilk help prop up, mustered a rearguard defense in the shape of the capitalist media, whose "imposed image of the good," to borrow Debord's language, "envelops in its spectacle the totality of what officially exists." William Solomon confirmed as much in the pages of *Monthly Review*. He noted how broadsheets like the *New York Times* and *Los Angeles Times* propagated a common ideological message: "Only zealots hold radical critiques of the WTO, which actually represents the best hope for the world's future."[50] Such demos, apparently, are "attributed solely to marginal figures who hold unconventional, impractical, and possibly unwise views." To put it bluntly, these protesters, the *New York Times* insists, are "a Noah's ark of flat-earth advocates."

BEYOND DYSTOPIA: BE REALISTIC,
DEMAND THE IMPOSSIBLE?

This sort of misrepresentation and flagrant distortion is the stuff of what Debord has more recently labeled the "integrated spectacle."[51] The integrated spectacle, he says, now brings together into a formidable reactionary force both "concentrated" and "diffuse" types of spectacle—the spectacle of dictatorship as well as "the Americanization of the world." The integrated spectacle lets nobody and nowhere off the hook. When the spectacle was concentrated, the greater part of surrounding society escaped it; when diffuse, a small part. Now, the integrated spectacle "permeates all reality." Its resounding accomplishments are "the globalization of the false and also the falsification of the globe." Its clarion call rings out loud and false as TINA—"There Is No Alternative." It's an end of history that "gives power a welcome break. Success is guaranteed in all its undertakings, or at least the rumor of success."[52] Should anybody try to challenge this power or any "agent of recuperation"—any Jeffery Sachs, Thomas Friedman, Alan Greenspan, Herbert Muschamp, any pinstripe, technocrat, or Third Wayer, any expert, consultant, or specialist—they're easily dismissed as idiotic, juvenile, naive. Listen up, wise up, grow up. There is no alternative.

And yet, "childish" pranks refuse to be quelled. "Immature" young people can still tell grown-ups a thing or two about mature life and politics. One of the crucial things that Debord and the Situationists still teach these immature young people—and a few older folk as well—is something that's hitherto disappeared: the notion that urbanism and politics can be *romantic*, can be full of ideals, mad raving ideals, that the future can be different, that we can *still believe in the future*. Even if these dreams and ideals never come true, at least they've kept the fire burning, glimmers of light shining, and hope alive.

Meanwhile, the interim journey will feel a lot more meaningful and richer—and who's to say those dreams won't come true anyway? Debord's critique of spectacular society anticipates the ideological manipulations of its ruling class as well as the direct action grassroots response. The disparate voices now coalescing around an oppositional lingua franca might have made Debord's heart soar. We will never know. At any rate, these different groups, with different agendas, pitched at different scales—canceling Third World debt, banning child and sweatshop labor, ridding cars from cities, keeping city life vital, taming unfettered globalization—are slowly clasping hands, out on the streets, especially as the batons flail. One day, maybe, they might come together for The Big One, for a great big global *détournement*. Wouldn't it be nice to see that ball drop in Times Square?

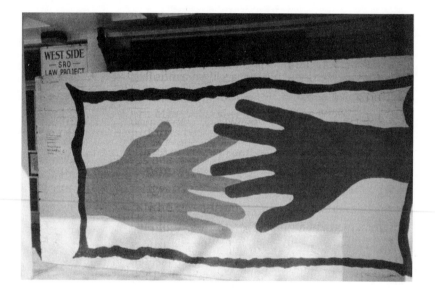

6

Lepers at the City Gate:
Single Room Occupancy and
New York's Housing Crisis

It's a sultry July morning, and I am sitting on a low wall outside a three-story brownstone at West 120th Street, a stone's throw away from Mount Morris Park, in Harlem. I am watching four workmen, all covered in dust and dirt, coming and going, throwing debris and masonry onto a nearby skip, cussing and bantering among themselves and disappearing into a gutted building, number 17. From my perch I can hear a lot of drilling and banging inside. Overhead, there's a lamp-post adorned with a banner welcoming you to Mount Morris Historic District, a patch bound by Lenox Avenue to the west, 124th Street to the north, 119th Street to the south, and Mount Morris Park to the east. (The park, which interrupts Fifth Avenue for a five-block stretch and is dominated by a craggy outcrop of rocks, was renamed Marcus Garvey Park in 1973, in honor of the Jamaican black nationalist.) My eyes follow a uniform row of redbrick and terra-cotta houses, most built around 1890, grand in their day, but many are now burnt-out shells, boarded up and abandoned. Wire railings seal several off; knee-high weeds and accumulated litter makes everything forlorn and menacing. I hear rustling and watch a disheveled black man, with two loaded bags, suddenly emerge from one ruin across the street.

As I ponder the scene a little longer, and look more closely at the fine detail, in the midst of the wreckage and dereliction I notice that a few structures actually look healthy. They have fine wooden shutters in their windows, have had their facades renovated and recent paint jobs, and have window boxes bearing fresh flowers. Telltale signs of change are in the air, a revival of sorts in Harlem, where, after years of neglect, properties are miraculously being spruced up, money is flowing back in after decades of flowing out, and people are returning, even middle-class people, both white and black. And, to cap it all, five blocks to the north, Starbucks, Gap, and Disney have each set up shop.

For the moment, I am early for an appointment with number 17's last tenant. It's amazing that somebody is still there, living in what looks like rubble. The workmen are unperturbed as I walk into the premises and go up the stairs in semidarkness. The atmosphere is thick with dust and I feel it catch my throat. At the top, a diminutive African-American woman, Mary Osborne, greets me, shakes my hand cheerily and ushers me into a second-floor room, welcoming me to her humble abode. It's barely 12 by 12 feet, though the tall ceilings help make it feel less claustrophobic. It's filled with her modest possessions: a small TV, a radio, a refrigerator, clothes stacked up on a single bed, all covered with plastic wrapping—"to protect everything from water leaks and the mess," Mary laments. In one corner there's a cheap bookshelf, upon which I spot Alex Haley's *Roots*, a biography of Malcolm X, several Bibles, a bulky treatise on Queen Elizabeth II, and, curiously, a paperback by a certain Donald Trump.

Mary has a mop of black curly hair, with only a couple of gray strands. She tells me she's fifty-four, yet somehow she looks ten years younger. She moved to New York in 1953, at the age of seven, with her longshoreman father, mother, and four siblings, migrating from rural South Carolina. They were poor, needless to say, and moved about a bit at first, several times in Harlem and then to Brooklyn, always into crummy apartments. "We had a lot of rats." She grins. "There are a lot of bad buildings in New York City."[1] Mary eventually returned to Harlem in her late teens and has been there, by herself, ever since, experiencing ups and downs, joy and pain, though lately more pain and downs. She worked once. That was before getting sick. Now Mary draws public assistance and represents a beleaguered and endangered species in the city. Mary is a single-room-occupancy (SRO) tenant, somebody who hasn't gained during the 1990s' boom times, nor is she ever likely to in the future. If anything, Mary and her ilk are directly threatened by such prosperity, by a thriving economy and buoyant real estate sector, which puts her whole livelihood on the brink. Nowadays, Harlem remains the last frontier of gentrification in Manhattan, a veritable beachhead north of 110th Street, and Mary knows she's being pushed into choppy seas, unable to swim.

A hundred years ago, Mary's neighborhood was genteel, one of Manhattan's most exclusive addresses; she'd have had no place in it then. Numerous New York City commissioners, mayors, captains of industry, rich merchants, physicians, and judges, to say nothing of Tammany Hall bosses, had gracious homes around Mount Morris Park. Upwardly mobile East European Jews, garment industry owners, spilling out of the Lower East Side, likewise established communities. Between 1878 and 1881, when elevated train lines reached 129th Street, investors jumped on the bandwagon, bought cheap land, sold it dear, made fortunes fast. Brownstones and exclusive apartments sprouted almost overnight and changed hands, always for higher prices. Harlem expanded phenomenally and optimistically. But in 1904–1905, inevitable bust struck and the speculative jamboree came to a whimpering halt. In the aftermath of financial collapse, poorer blacks moved uptown, 50,000 by 1914.[2] In 1920, two-thirds of Manhattan's black community lived in Harlem. Before long, scores of black writers, artists, musicians, scholars, bohemians, and political activists found Harlem, and Harlem found them. Whites suddenly discovered Bessie Smith and Josephine Baker, "exotic" jazz and blues nightspots, black literature and thought, and overcame a few stereotypes as they reinforced others. Alas, the Depression abruptly ended Harlem's Renaissance.

The neighborhood endured thereafter as an appalling slum. Drugs and arson became typical growth sectors in recent decades; a lot of landlords and homeowners burned down their properties to cash in on fire insurance; other businesses and properties bore the brunt of redlining and "benign neglect"; still more neighborhoods perished through the "planned shrinkage" of essential services. After the mid-1970s, asserting "in rem" legal action, the city took charge of thousands of abandoned properties for nonpayment of taxes. A few wily speculators bought buildings at fire sale prices from the city or from owners who wanted to sell. Then they simply sat tight, paid taxes but skimped on repairs and services, and prospered from perpetuating deterioration.

But now that Harlem real estate has perked up, big gains are in the offing: buildings purchased for under $150,000 sell for between $600,000 and $750,000. Peanuts by Midtown standards, but prices go on rising rapidly, and middle-class people are capitalizing on these bargains; even wrecked brownstones now fetch $300,000. Doubtless New Yorkers should be glad about this upward swing, about Harlem's latest Renaissance, yet it has a darker side, frequently forgotten and occasionally ignored, amid the clamor of boosterism and triumphalism.

"I've been here since 1993," Mary tells me. "I was living at 121st Street until the old owner died and the new one started tearing everything down around me." She wanted Mary out of the single room. At first, Mary refused to budge. Then the owner started "doing harassment." Mary didn't want trouble; she finally gave in and fled. "I wasn't really happy, but a neighborhood friend of mine found me this room. There was nothing better." Her father bought her a refrigerator and changed the locks, her brother applied a coat of paint. "Being poor, I tried to make it comfortable." But after that owner died, things started to deteriorate. The latest landlord, a local entrepreneur, had big plans for his Harlem property. The eleven units would be renovated, adjoining walls knocked down on every floor, combining rooms, installing new toilets and kitchens, and transforming dingy rooms into plush one- and two-bedroom apartments, with rents beginning at $2,000 per month. All existing tenants—Mary, a middle-aged black man, and three Ecuadorian families—had to vacate, immediately. "It was a Sunday evening, around seven-thirty, October 1999. No warning, no letter, no nothing, just 'boom, boom, boom!' at the door." Three mighty fellows stood there and gave Mary a week's notice. Seemingly overnight, the other tenants disappeared. Now Mary finds herself alone. She feels like she's "walking in the wilderness": "I'm the last leaf on a lonely tree. I hope that if the wind blows me off, it blows me off to a special place." In the summer of 2000, Mary met one of her former neighbors again, shopping on 125th Street, a Latina with her little girl. "They said they're in a shelter. I asked them, 'Why did you move? I don't know, don't know,' she answers. They don't understand the court system," Mary says, "they don't understand their rights."

Single-room-occupancy units are one of New York's most important reserves of affordable housing for single adults on fixed incomes or with limited resources. Often they are last-resort housing for people whose annual earnings seldom top $10,000. Manhattan has over three-quarters of the city's stock, many in large, prewar apartment hotels, though Harlem has the densest concentration, frequently in lowrise rooming and townhouses. SROs are really a longstanding institution, dating back to World War I, when ex-servicemen with no families to return to found a grubby haven. The stock likewise provided cheap and safe shelter for lone women, struggling artists, and factory workers, or for anybody else who sought the city's bright lights and good life. Residents then as now inhabit one room with meager furniture, usually sharing bathroom and kitchen facilities with fellow occupants along the hall. Oftentimes a sense of community prevailed; sometimes it still does—despite the shabbiness. Throughout the 1950s, there were around 200,000 SRO units in Gotham. During the next three decades, the stock steadily shed numbers. Since the early 1980s, decline has been dramatic. In 1986, only 64,000 units clung on. By 1996, less than 47,000 had withstood free-market onslaught. At the beginning of the new century, it's estimated that fewer than 40,000 survive. Before this decade is done, the species may well be extinct.

Historically, SRO tenants have had certain rights under New York's Rent Stabilization Code. But there are "transiency loopholes," and stabilization laws continue to be flouted. For example, hotel and rooming house owners can legally charge whatever they want for the first six months of a tenant's occupancy. Thereafter, rent is supposed to be lowered to the stabilized level and the resident effectively becomes "permanent." Still, in practice, as long as SRO tenants remain ignorant of this law, landlords can—and invariably do—charge what they like. The rent code, meanwhile, requires that landlords provide a tenant with a "Notice of Rights and Duties," a formal contract detailing the precise status of their permanent tenancy and safeguards protecting them from illegal eviction.

Mary has gotten wise about her rights over the past few months, learning the hard way. "I'm trying my best to fight for my rights as an SRO tenant," she says, resolutely. "I'm hoping we can work something out, something comparable, because I'm stuck between a rock and a hard place right now." She explains that she gets $215 per month federal shelter allowance, plus a further $68 toward her nine kinds of medication. She's hyperglycemic and has hypertension and high cholesterol. She actually pays $60 per week on rent, contributing $25 of her own income. "I don't really live off anything too much. It's been a harsh struggle." For a while she hustled as a post office temp. "Everyday they'd send you to a different area. Some days they put me on the truck dragging sacks. Before long my body started to break down." At that time Mary was also taking night classes at John Jay College, doing six credits each semester in criminal justice, but after seven years she couldn't afford the tuition hikes. "I got disgusted and just gave up. But I'd love to go back. I like to read a lot of spirituality books now and try to read something that keeps me going, gives me self-confidence, shows me how to plant seeds and be prosperous. It doesn't have to be money or something of value. The landlords I've encountered don't have no feelings; it's all about money, profit and gain."

Since March 2000, it's been difficult for Mary to pursue her regular reading regime. "Drilling and banging all night," she says. The workmen are busy around the clock, coming in the morning and leaving practically at dawn, with hardly any respite. She can't sleep, "I can't do nothing. They got paint in the bathtub and the toilet is all blocked up and doesn't flush. They even took the toilet seat away. Now I have to go to the store around the corner where they have a bathroom." In November 1999, a lot of Mary's clothes were damaged in a water leak. The ceiling of her kitchenette, about the size of a small closet, caved in after workers labored in the apartment above. There were loud bangs and vibrations and, suddenly, water came gushing though the light fixture, drenching everything. She had to phone the fire brigade who turned off the water mains and electricity. "Didn't have either all weekend." Mary encourages me to inspect the scene for myself. I peer into a little alcove and sure enough see an old, grease-stained cooker, and a badly cracked and yellowed ceiling, with a single bare lightbulb. "There was a rat running around as well," she adds matter-of-factly "Came in through a hole in the kitchen. He was like a little kitten. So I started walking 'round in boots. I was too scared to even eat or sleep. I could hear him moving like a human being." It was then that Mary accused her landlord of harassment and started to act. Mary sought guidance from Harlem's legal aid services on 125th Street, which holds a clinic every Tuesday. These days, she says, it has its work cut out with tenant grumbles and you have to arrive there early to avoid a long wait. The legal aid people recommended that Mary consult the West Side SRO Law Project, a more specialized tenant advocacy and advisory organization, whose offices are at the Goddard-Riverside Community Center on the Upper West Side. Mary didn't waste any time. "They've been very effective at trying to help me."

ORGANIZING FOR ACTION:
SRO TENANTS UNITE!

The Law Project occupies a cramped, ground-floor office at Columbus Avenue between 91st and 92nd Streets. The community center itself, shadowed by a twenty-story apartment complex, is a hive of activity, bustling with T-shirt-clad white, black, and Hispanic youth attending a summer day camp. At the entrance outside, there's a large mural, painted by neighborhood kids, of two outstretched hands, one yellow, another brown. The different colored fingers just about make contact. Inside, beyond the Law Project's threshold, it's a good deal quieter, even though the phone is constantly ringing. Staff carrying documents hurry by me. Flyers festoon notice boards. A couple proclaim, "SRO TENANTS UNITED!" and "SROTU PLANS NEW OUTREACH CAMPAIGN." Another says, "ORGANIZE FOR ACTION!" It's August 2000 and I am here to visit Terry Poe, one of four tenant organizers, and Elizabeth Kane, the project's director. Sitting in his tiny, neat office, Poe, who's in his fifties, says he grew up in Louisiana, became radicalized as an antiwar activist in the 1960s, and once taught history in Massachusetts and did a stint as a labor organizer for the Service Employees International Union in Boston. Since 1989, he's been trying to organize SRO tenants in New York.

The Law Project, he says, was originally conceived back in 1981 in response to the alarming decline of SROs and recognition that New York's burgeoning homelessness crisis could be traced to the loss of such housing. On the Upper West Side especially, many owners wanted to convert their large SRO buildings into either glitzy condos or upscale co-ops. En route, a lot of tenants lost their heating, hot water, and elevator service, or were strong-armed by thugs and intimidated by drug dealers and prostitutes, who, Poe thinks, were purposely recruited to rid buildings of rent stabilized tenants. There were suspicious fires in buildings, too, and tenants were often beaten up and robbed. Little wonder that the media had a field day, christening the area "the Wild West." Goddard-Riverside Community Center felt obliged to intervene. They rallied against the bad press and worked with other local associations and community groups to petition the City, demanding that they respond more effectively to preserve SRO stock. Out of this agitation came the Law Project, founded and funded by the Department of Housing Preservation and Development (HPD).

Elizabeth Kane describes the project's birth pangs and growing pains. She's an attorney in her mid-forties, somebody who's wanted to help low-income people since law school. "I knew then I wanted to be involved in civil rights or constitutional law or in some way be a public service lawyer. It was never my interest to work in the corporate world, never my interest to make the rich richer."[3] She's adamant that in the 1970s New York demonstrated its intent to destroy SRO buildings. An amendment to J-51 coding in 1975, for one thing, actually provided subsidies and tax breaks to any owner or developer who undertook upscale reconversion. Ridding the city of SROs, replacing them with higher-order uses, somehow made sound sense. After all, it brought a lot of money to the city: developers and construction companies hire workers, make healthy profits; landlords reap rewards; communities see scruffy, old, problematical buildings, full of problematical people, gentrified; and, to top it all, the city's tax base is expanded. "It seemed lovely to everyone," Kane says. "Except for the obvious: if you destroy the housing of your low-income people where are they to go? In 1981, New York City sort of looked down and said, 'Oh my gosh, we now have this huge homeless population that we didn't have just a few years ago, where did this come from, how did it happen?'" So the city finally began to confront what was already obvious to many. "One of the things we point out to the city every year when we go down to City Hall to beg and plead for our funding," Kane concedes, with a tinge of cynicism, "is that we're a lot cheaper than the cost of homelessness. It cost somewhere around $20,000 a year to house a single adult in a shelter. This project has been funded at under $500,000 a year and prevents a lot of people from becoming homeless. The math is fairly simple: it's a lot more economical to pay us."

A decade on, the Law Project provides free legal representation of SRO tenants in the housing court and offers advice about how they can defend themselves before legislative bodies. Since 1996, a new organizing campaign, SRO Tenants United! has tried to ratchet up the fight against landlord harassment, rent overcharge, illegal eviction and construction, and has extended its activities deeper into Harlem. In the process, it's been running community education workshops and outreach programs, as well as monthly tenant meetings, to publicize the loss of affordable housing and destruction of inveterate mixed communities. "The irony," Terry Poe admits, "is we're fighting to defend private-sector, market-led, housing. It's really a rearguard action. We're trying to make preferential options for the poor. There's no affordable housing being built in the city anymore. In the face of no alternative, SROs must be defended. They're last resort housing, but they needn't be."[4]

Although New York's population grew 350,000 between 1981 and 1999, it added just 42,000 new rental units.[5] With demand far exceeding supply, and with a relatively dwindling stock and low vacancy rate, rents have risen a lot, unsurprisingly. Since 1975, median rents jumped 33 percent while median incomes, adjusted for inflation, grew 3 percent. The waiting list for public housing currently tops 130,000 families, and shelters are stretched beyond coping on typical nights. Despite record budget surpluses and eight years of unprecedented economic expansion and prosperity, nobody in the late 1990s seemed bothered about building affordable housing. Money talks, for sure, but it equally votes with its feet, seeks out its best interests, and low-income housing plainly isn't one of them. Poe knows that context forces the project's back against the wall. And yet, he remains stoical about what needs to be done, about what doing the right thing means. He smiles at me and cites Ezra Pound's *Cantos*: "'The blossoms of Apricot blow from east to west, / And I have tried to keep them from falling.' It's a verse," says Poe, "that every once in a while when I'm feeling particularly sorry for myself I think of."

Poe and Kane agree New York's steady rightward shift under Giuliani made their life and job a lot tougher. "It's depressing, it's hard, it's draining," Kane says. "I feel I expend so much energy, both psychologically and physically, dealing with the bleak political atmosphere that we function in as much as I do directly providing services for tenants. Giuliani wasn't interested in preserving low-income housing, he's not interested in preserving opportunities for low-income people to live in this city." Kane insists that her clients now have more difficulty with immigration issues and with welfare: "They're not able to get the same benefits, not able to get food stamps, not able to switch to social security when it's appropriate. All of that, of course, makes the housing situation more difficult."

In early 1999, the Law Project and the 6th District's Democratic councilwoman Ronnie Eldridge drafted a more definitive tenant protection bill, so-called Intro 108, which, if passed, would have compelled the Department of Buildings (DOB) to halt unauthorized construction work, immediately imposing "Stop Work" orders. The bill would have equally sent a message that people are favored over profits and that the progressive expulsion of low-income dwellers from the island of Manhattan needs deterring. But the proposed measure received a lukewarm reaction in official circles and was never enacted. Instead, flimsy harassment laws prevail in the city; savvy landlords and developers with time and money can easily circumvent them. Since 1983, would-be building converters can obtain a work permit only if they've first gotten a "Certificate of No Harassment." This involves an official inquiry, determining whether they've had a record of harassment in the three years prior to their application. If they're clean, they get a green light. "The mechanism," Kane says, "tries to make it not so economically worthwhile for landlords to harass tenants out of the building." Nevertheless, landlords with future renovation plans can simply lie low, wait for three years, proceed as if nothing is happening, butter up their tenants, be obliging about maintenance and service provision, even, as some have, give out Christmas gifts—until, of course, they receive the necessary certificate.

"The minute landlords get the Certificate of No Harassment and work permit," Kane argues, "they use the construction itself to try to drive out tenants." She thinks the law should be amended to cover at least a five-year stretch, "and if landlords have a history of harassment elsewhere, this should be taken into account, too." Even when work is carried out illegally, without a permit, it's seldom stopped quickly enough, if it's stopped at all. "A 'Stop Work' order may be issued, but what then?" Kane sighs. "The city doesn't follow up in a meaningful way." Landlords apparently pile up reprimands like parking tickets, and they're well able to pay the measly fines. Meanwhile, the SRO unit within the Department of Housing Preservation and Development (HPD) litigation bureau has recently been liquidated; SRO litigation is now handled by attorneys with little expertise or interest is SRO issues. Moreover, the Code Enforcement Unit within the city's Corporation

Counsel has been axed, leaving the city without specialized staff for the prosecution of building code violations.

According to HPD data, the number of legal building conversions in New York rose from 82 in 1993 to 140 in 1997, affecting 1,683 units as opposed to 568. Figures for shady renovations aren't known exactly, though the West Side Law Project estimates that the number of SRO units illegally converted into non-SRO usage easily matches the number of legal conversions. Between 1996 and 1997, the number of applications for Certificates of No Harassment grew 40 percent at the city scale and 35 percent for Harlem. Harlem is clearly an untapped reservoir of speculative redevelopment, but it's also a traditional source of low-income housing. Unfortunately, right now these two characteristics duel with each other. Indeed, there are 733 SRO buildings in the area between 119th and 121st Streets and 5th and 7th Avenues, containing roughly 9,500 units. In the twelve-block patch between 119th and 121st Streets, there are nearly 300 buildings with about 3,500 units—and all are seemingly fair game. As the Law Project states in a bright-colored flyer, "The rapid gentrification of some areas of Harlem—continually being championed by the *New York Times*—has led to the displacement of many rooming house tenants by new owners who seek to convert their SROs into apartment or single family homes, or who just want to empty out the buildings and resell them at a huge profit."

One particular property, the Park View Hotel, slightly farther south at West 110th Street and Lenox, has undergone another kind of conversion: into a tourist hostel. "Yesterday, a Grimy S.R.O," the *New York Times* boasted in a June 25, 2000, headline, "Today, a Tourists' Haven." "Once a landing pad for West African immigrants," the article goes on, "the hotel provided an enduring, if bitter, first impression of New York. . . . Recent arrivals worked as taxi drivers, street vendors and students, trying to climb the rungs of New York's economic ladder to escape the grimy gray single-room-occupancy hotel, which they shared with a handful of native New Yorkers, many of them welfare recipients." The *Times* urges us to "fast forward five years." Now, miraculously, the building is somehow "a refurbished youth hostel. . . . painted in vibrant blues, oranges, and yellows and has large leatherette ottomans dispersed around low-lying tables." Clerks at the front desk "wearing matching orange suits, chirpily greet arriving guests from France or England." Five years on we hear no mention of what happened to those

West African immigrants, to those cabbies and street vendors, no inkling as to where they went? Elizabeth Kane slows down the image for us and provides a bit more clarity: during the eight-month renovation, she suggests, "many tenants were brutally treated and driven out of the building."

There are further, bigger, fears for about 350 brownstones in Central Harlem—90 percent of which are likely to be SROs—because they've been facing imminent mortgage foreclosure. These properties are part of a highly controversial federal loan scheme, the Department of Housing and Urban Development's (HUD) federal Rehabilitation Mortgage Insurance, Section 203(k). Originally, the "203(k) program" had an honorable intent: to promote homeownership for poor and moderate-income people and to help certain nonprofits in neighborhood restoration. Bankers and financiers provided mortgages of up to $400,000 toward house purchase and rehab in neighborhoods and for people otherwise deemed to be risky bets. Under the scheme, HUD simply underwrote all risk. Should the buyer default, the Federal Housing Administration (FDA) steps in, guaranteeing the lender's money back, plus all costs incurred. In and around New York City, there were 134 such loans made in 1996. In 1998, numbers exploded to 1,128. Still, quite early on HUD's auditors smelled a rat, rightly suspecting the program "highly vulnerable to waste, fraud and abuse by investors and nonprofit borrowers." As it transpired, appraisers did indeed get carried away and persistently overvalued property; nonprofits, too, were eventually overwhelmed by covert for-profits, while contractors, realtors and brokers creamed off exorbitant fees. In a nutshell, the 203(k) program became rich pickings for the wrong sort of people.[6]

The scam has lately besieged Central Harlem, where "mortgage lenders have been aggressively pushing to sell these properties to nonprofits. But what's been typically happening," Terry Poe explains, "is that they've been getting these high mortgages and not putting any money into the building, not doing any intended rehabilitation. Now, the banks and mortgage companies are foreclosing." Nobody really seems to know the true extent and depth of abuse and finagling, and in early 2002 a criminal investigation was still going on. Poe worries that this is "a huge scandal" and it "may potentially have a major impact on SROs in Central Harlem." One broker he spoke with has already sent out a list of 114 properties fresh on the market. "I guess all the mortgage lenders must have gotten together," Poe speculates, "and hired brokers to try to get rid of the buildings before they're foreclosed on. If it happens," he warns, "and the buildings are foreclosed on, or if they go to auction or a receiver is appointed, it's going to be very serious for the tenants. Either somebody with absolutely no interest in running the building as housing will buy them, just milk them and sell them again, or somebody will buy them up, try to push the tenants out, renovate them, and sell them for more money."

So far, in HUD's inquiry, 33 people have been arrested and 19 have admitted guilt.[7] Then-secretary of HUD, Andrew Cuomo, subsequently a candidate for governor of New York, pledged to rebuild those SRO properties in Harlem (and in Brooklyn and the Bronx) quagmired in 203(k) default. He wants to turn a tragedy into an opportunity, he said, and use federal money to bail out more than $70 million of taxpayers' cash that's already been filched by real estate villains.[8] Meanwhile, the West Side Law Project braces itself for a wholesale emptying out of 203(k)-related SRO buildings in Central and Lower Harlem. There is a slim hope that HUD's response will permit some tenants to stay put after their properties undergo renovation—renovation that was never done first time around. Yet, as a SRO Tenants United! newsletter pointed out in April 2001, "The 203(k) loan scam may cost the federal government tens of millions of dollars, but tenants living in the abandoned buildings pay the real price."

In March 2001, SRO residents at a West 132nd Street building reached the end of their tether. After a decidedly chilly winter without heating, they held a street rally with fellow SRO folk in Harlem, protesting HUD's failure to pay a Con Edison electricity bill. Next day, electricity was restored, and the day after that, they finally got their heat back.

WEST SIDE TENANTS ON THE VERGE

On the Upper West Side, meanwhile, other SRO tenants grumbled about another practice that's surfaced only relatively recently. They said they'd suffered harassment at the hands of landlords intent on transforming their buildings into tourist rentals. Elizabeth Kane identifies this as an emerging and threatening trend: "Gentrification," she explained to me, "had slowed down in the 1980s. It wasn't quite what it had been in the 1970s and it wasn't what it is now. Now, of course, it's slightly different—

it's not gentrification for people in the city, it's not converting a SRO to serve Yuppies with high incomes. Now it's tourism. The tourist boom is the driving force behind it."[9] Two tenants, Leah Porter and Grace Gross, longtime residents at 222 West 77th Street, a big prewar building overlooking Broadway, have lived through the fallout of this ongoing boom. They're angry about it, and are willing to talk. They suggest I stop by, and they'll fill me in on the graphic details, recount typical tales of woe.

NYC & Company, the city's convention and visitors' bureau, estimates that an unprecedented 36.7 million tourists and business travelers flocked to the Big Apple in 1999, a figure bettered only by Orlando, and 11 percent more than the previous year.[10] These people spent $15 billion at hotels, stores, restaurants and cultural attractions. That spending, in turn, supposedly generated $2.9 billion in local, state and federal tax revenues, and supports 275,000 jobs. To accommodate this visitor hike, the city added 1,000 new rooms in 1999, and 3,000 more are in the pipeline. Meanwhile, guest rooms continue to sell at ultra-high prices: 2000's average was $220 a day, the most expensive in the nation, double what it was a decade ago.[11]

There are downsides to this boom, needless to say. One is simply overcrowding, greater vehicular and pedestrian traffic and congestion in the street and on the sidewalk. Another is the specter of overspeculation and overbuilding, a lesson learned from the early 1990s' slump, when lots of hoteliers and investors badly burned their fingers and slashed room prices and defaulted on debts. (These circumstances, on the other hand, might actually prove propitious for SRO tenants since it releases displacement pressures and forces rents down.) A third contradiction confronts the city's planners, politicos, and policy pundits. New York's extrovert, cosmopolitan nature, a place open to the world and a magnet for visitors and travelers, is increasingly threatening its own neighborhood character, its traditional hometown status, its role as a place where ordinary folks eke out a living.

The building at 222 West 77th Street embodies this latter tension. It has an interesting, albeit checkered, past. In a sense, the building's fortunes over the years directly mirror the fortunes of the Upper West Side and New York itself: it's an unlikely barometer whose dial has fluctuated as the city and the neighborhood has blown cold and hot. In 1976, when Leah Porter first moved in, the building, known then as the Benjamin Franklin Hotel, was a somewhat shabby and cheap residential hotel, full of single-room-occupants, working people like Leah, who were just about making out. After awhile, the SRO became the Broadway American. Today, after a costly facelift and rehab, the old Broadway American is now the new On the Ave, a midpriced, short-stay boutique hotel, with standard rooms beginning at $240 per night. The lobby still smells of recent renovation. It's a modern, open-plan design, with a slight Zen-minimalist feel. The air conditioning is chilly and Muzak pipes out softly. Nobody impedes my passage as I take the elevator up to the eighth floor. The hotel's glossy and cliché-laden brochure boasts: "Like the famed restaurants and shops that distinguish the Upper West Side, ON THE AVE epitomizes its neighborhood. Its very essence is rich with the Manhattan qualities that New Yorkers experience every day of their lives—and with the service and features expected of a leading hotel. . . . ON THE AVE's meticulously decorated rooms present striking furnishings in an environment rich with texture and light. From the innovative lobby-salon to the distinctive guest rooms, ON THE AVE has refined the hotel stay in New York."

Leah Porter, who's white and sixty-three, lives in room 826, and is one of seventy or so remaining permanent tenants at the hotel. She invites me into her prim oblong home, measuring about 8 by 15 feet, with a wash basin in the corner. It's decorated with floral curtains and her divan bed acts as a sofa by day. The place looks and feels like a regular apartment living room. As we sip iced tea and talk, Leah's neighbor, Grace Gross, an African-American woman maybe ten years Leah's junior, joins us. Before long, the conversation flows. "We've had a lot of different owners," Leah tells me. "But when I first moved into the building, one elderly gentleman owned it and you had to be interviewed to make sure that you were respectable, to make sure that you took care of yourself."[12] Leah was thirty-something then, "definitely one of the younger ones." She says the neighborhood was frayed and the building shabby—but clean and safe. "It was so safe here that in the summer, because I didn't have air conditioning, I slept with my door wide open. We all did. Nothing was ever stolen. I remember telling my mother, 'You cannot believe this place I've found. It's a little oasis of peace and safety and tranquillity.' It was a godsend, it was a lifesaver for me." Leah paid $36 a week, sold cosmetics for Elizabeth Arden, and was trying to pick up the pieces of her life after a failed marriage. (Leah pays $239 per month now, suffers from depression, and no longer works. She's been receiving welfare and food stamps since 1988.)

Grace arrived in 1981, paid more, but with her steady bank job it was affordable. She continues to work for a bank and currently pays about $430 a month. (Her room, I discover for myself later, is big, bright, and attractive, about twice the size of Leah's, full of plants, and with a lovely bird's-eye view over Broadway.) "The place was still shabby," Grace says, "but very clean and quiet, and there was always somebody down at the desk. If they didn't know you, they would stop you, ask you who you were and where you were going." "Unfortunately," Leah chips in, "the character of the building started to get run-down." Apparently, it started to change hands fast after the old owner died. First came the Crowns. "They kept breaking the bathroom windows in the winter. We'd put cardboard up and they'd rip it down. We'd never have heat or hot water," Leah remembers. "It was bleak. They eventually had their license taken away and could no longer operate."

Then the Goldmans took over, in 1980, Leah thinks. "They wanted to sell and wanted us out. They wanted richer people in. But we told them we weren't moving, that we had no place else to go. So they started putting in prostitutes and drug dealers and dangerous people, starting using terror tactics. They started charging illegal rents like $175 per week. The building next door was a welfare hotel and they'd be throwing things out of the window. I got pushed around every time I passed. You couldn't walk by late at night. You'd hear screaming inside, and they'd yell and carry on. Amsterdam Avenue wasn't that safe, neither was Columbus, especially after dark." Leah says things in and around her building weren't very nice. "The point was that it wasn't supposed to be as nice. We were supposed to leave." So a fledgling West Side SRO Law Project stepped in and took class action proceedings. Then, says Leah, events quieted down for a while and it "wasn't so bad." Permanent SRO folks weren't about to go anywhere. In fact, because their numbers at the time comprised at least 70 percent of all tenants at the Broadway American, state and city laws deem them rent controlled. Legally, too, they cannot be moved.

And yet, as they stayed put, the environment around them became steadily tonier and tonier. Up and down Broadway, between 72nd and 112th Streets, former SRO buildings have been picked off, one by one. Apartments that once rented for a couple hundred a month were suddenly sold for more than half a million dollars. Shabby gentility has given way to nouveau riche chic. "It was a neighborhood then," Grace reminisces. "Now, it's yuppie, duppie, $2,000-plus rents. I always felt that when I went outside I was walking with people who were like me. You know, who were just getting the rent check written every month. Now, when you go out you know it's not like that. You feel like you're an outsider. It's so money oriented—where if it was before, you didn't feel it. It's a whole 'nother world out there now."

"Fifteen years ago," Leah insists, "they would never have considered opening a Food Emporium. We can't afford to shop there. We still end up going to the Met on Eighty-sixth Street. We no longer feel that we're welcomed. Please leave! Well, we were here when you couldn't go out after dark!" For Grace and Leah, that old, jaded, and slightly menacing residential neighborhood now feels overbuilt and overcrowded. They can't hide their nostalgia. "Sometimes," Leah says, "you feel like you're on Fifth Avenue, you can't walk on the streets, they're so crowded. It's become so posh." I asked Leah what being a SRO tenant meant to her: "It means independence," she responded, without hesitation. "It was wonderful. This used to be a residential neighborhood. It was our home and they're taking it away."

Judgment Day arrived at the Broadway American in April 1997 when a new, youngish, and ambitious New York real estate investment company, Property Markets Group (PMG), bought the building for $20 million. Immediately, PMG committed itself to a $12 million overhaul, taking what they perceived to be a grossly undercapitalized property in a state of disrepair, fix it up, and then rent out the rooms to transient higher bidders. Citylife Hotel Group, a division of PMG, would run operations and manage the new creation. (Citylife, incidentally, also controls the Habitat Hotel on East 57th Street, formerly the Allerton Hotel (SRO), the Hotel Thirty-Thirty on East 29th Street, formerly the Martha Washington Hotel (SRO), and the Commander Hotel (SRO) on West 73rd Street.) By January 1998, the rehab had begun at the top and was working its way down. In early March, it had reached Leah and Grace's floor. "They wanted us to move downstairs," Leah recalls. "They said they'd give us a larger room with a bathroom."

But Leah and Grace were suspicious: they didn't trust PMG. Terry Poe told them not to trust PMG, too. The room they offered would have been facing an alley and darker; moreover, it was nearer the front door. It was really a ploy to edge us out, Leah felt: "Some of our friends on the eighth floor moved. We pleaded with them not to go. Every single one of them since has said, 'We should have listened to you.' It's like it's three different hotels now. There are us and the tourists and the people downstairs. With some elderly tenants, PMG moved them down and then shifted them out. They called up social services and said these people can't look after themselves anymore. It was a lie." For two years, daily life was a dread-zone building site. There was no hot water or heating, the floor was gutted, dust and debris lay everywhere, with endless thumping and drilling, even at weekends—especially at weekends. Builders blocked up the windows, submerging everything in eerie darkness. One Saturday, Grace recalls, she and Leah had had enough. Both decided to stage a sit-in to physically block construction. They donned their tattiest clothes and wouldn't budge from the corridor. They halted work for that day. Eventually, the workmen—read: nonunion workmen; PMG are also union busters—who claimed not to speak English, relented. It was a minor moral victory. "PMG made the construction as loud as possible, as dirty as possible, with as much harassment as possible," Leah believes. "They really never thought that the few of us who stayed on would be able to stick it through." "On the Ave, yeah, sure. 'On the Verge' more like," Grace jokes, with vintage gallows humor.

Elizabeth Kane corroborates this Piranesian nightmare. "At the Broadway American," she told me, "they were clearly trying to get tenants out and went about it in a very brutal fashion. Tenants lived through really horrible conditions and didn't cave. At their request, we initiated a civil suit against the landlord for damages based on the 'warranty of habitability.'" The case against Property Markets Group, Kane admits, "is plodding its way very, very slowly through the [state supreme] court system, in part because the landlord would like to take it as long as possible. What will come from that suit we have yet to see. Hopefully, there will be some real compensation." Property Markets Group, the brainchild of Kevin Maloney, an ex-banker, Ziel Feldman, a real estate lawyer, and David Bernstein, a hotelier, did actually receive a Certificate of No Harassment for its conversion of On the Ave. Since then, however, it's stridently violated tenants' rights and has become one of Manhattan's most aggressive hotel converters. Presently, they control about seventy-five rent-controlled buildings in New York. At the Commander Hotel, for instance, dozens of harassment charges and grievances were filed in early 1998 against the company.

In fact, these allegations, all subsequently substantiated, helped scupper PMG's activities at the Allerton, once a genteel residential hotel for young ladies, built in the early 1920s. (In its heyday, the Allerton used to have a marble staircase, a grand piano in the lobby, and wouldn't allow men above the third floor.) HPD denied PMG a Certificate of No Harassment in February 1999. Company executives pressed city housing officials to overrule the verdict—unsuccessfully. Now, the hotel management sits out a three-year ban, able to carry out only renovations that don't alter unit numbers or dramatically reconfigure rooms. Meantime, Citylife pleads innocence, saying it signed a 49-year lease of the hotel in mid-1997. Tenant harassment, they argue, occurred prior to this date, under the old ownership, not theirs. In principle, reconversion at the Allerton immediately had to stop. In reality, PMG, like many other hotel converters in New York's lucrative tourist trade, carry on regardless.

One such operator and illegal converter is the notorious Sam Domb, once described as "the pompadoured operator of seedy SRO hotels." He's also listed as a major fund-raiser for Rudolph Giuliani, as well as the ex-mayor's close friend. Domb gained national notoriety in 1993 when he engineered a White House photo op between a Russian plutonium smuggler and Bill Clinton! In New York, Sam and his side-kick son, Jay, drew similar attention, and were on the wrong side of a lawsuit at the Simmons House on West 88th Street near Riverside Drive, a former women's refuge. Now the Riverside Hotel, the Dombs started illegally renovating the 175-unit complex in 1994, violating city building codes and zoning laws. Domb Sr., however, passed the buck over to hotel manager Jay, who created mayhem for tenants: elevators were perpetually out of order, bathrooms ripped out, water and electricity cut off.

Construction sought to drive residents crazy and force them out. Workers drew lewd pictures on walls; hotel staff frequently propositioned female tenants for sex, sometimes in exchange for their mail. In September 1998, a twenty-nine-year-old woman, Pamela Tewes, could suffer no more hammering, harassment, and late-night tourist reveling; she took a death tumble out of a five-floor window. (Another resident, incidentally, had leapt out of a seventh-floor kitchen window when construction began. Somebody else took a fatal dive from the same window in late 1998.) Tragedies aside, the Law Project actually views their Simmons House campaign in a favorable light. For one thing, they did gain "Stop Work" orders. For another, as Terry Poe points out, "We kept 53 out of 150 SRO units. So we saved about a third of the rooms for permanent tenants for a period of up to twenty years. After that, all bets are off. We also negotiated eighteen months' rent abatement. We lost two-thirds of the rooms, but we'd probably consider that a success."

The Law Project suspects that Sam and Jay Domb lurk somewhere behind the scenes of ongoing conversions at the six large SRO hotels sandwiched between Riverside Drive and West End Avenue: the Devon, Montroyal, and St. Louis on 94th Street, and the Pennington, Camden, and Continental on 95th. All told, these conversions comprise 972 units, of which roughly two-thirds are believed to be SRO. Several properties here are owned by well-known Domb acquaintances, Nick Gavalas and Scott Norych, who are antagonists in the project's latest tenant organizing drive, which is now being initiated with their perennial pessimism of the intellect and optimism of the will. "If we follow the Simmons House model," Poe concedes, "what we will accomplish here is forcing landlords to retain some rooms for permanent residents while they're allowed to convert others into tourist use. We can only try to stop the floodgates from opening." In real numbers, the homes of about six hundred low-income people are at threat. However, for the foreseeable future, such defensive maneuvering is as good as it gets. Many displaced people will doubtless return to live with family or friends, if they have any; some, if they're lucky, may find alternative cheap housing; a lot more are likely to end up in shelters; and a few will find their way onto the street. One day, Poe and his Law Project colleagues hope for a real political commitment of resources toward affordable, single-person accommodation, probably not SROs, but studio apartments with kitchenettes and bathrooms. For the time being, "we see no such commitment," Poe says. "We're not going to have a commitment to any sort of program that benefits poor working-class people in this town."

As I depart from the Law Project's offices, I glance back at that colorful mural, those two almost-clasping hands. Then I remember Mary Osborne, sitting in her little room in Harlem amid the rubble, wondering where she might go next, thinking about whose hand she might clasp. Something Mary had said lingers in me. She'd cited from her

Bible, from the Old Testament Book of Kings 2, chapter 7, the parable of "lepers at the city gate." Four leprous men, Mary explained, deliberate. "Why should we sit here until we die? If we decide to go into the city, we shall die there, for there is famine in the city. If we remain here, we shall die, too." Of course, the lepers have really nothing to lose, in some ways like Mary. So they decide to act, decide to go to the camp of the Arameans. "If they spare us, we live; if they kill us, we die." The lepers can't know the outcome in advance. As it happens, when the men reach the camp, no one was there. They live, and eat food, drink, and clothe themselves. Their activism somehow saved them; it would have saved them even if they had lost. Mary finds inspiration here: "I, too, am entering the city," she said. "We SRO tenants are lepers at the gate of Giuliani's New York. 'Why should we sit here and die?'"

7

Two-fold Urbanism:
A Negative Dialectic
of the City

ROSES ARE PLANTED WHERE THORNS GROW. |

AND ON THE BARREN HEATH | SING THE HONEY BEES.

—William Blake, "The Marriage of Heaven and Hell"

The city fulfills a functional role within the capitalist system. Cities, after all, help expand and socialize the productive forces, are the foundation of the division of labor, reign as seats of government and power, exhibit class distinctions and residential ghettoizations, and bear the imprint of geographical uneven development. As such, cities operate as vital nerve centers of the mode of production itself. They permit the exchange and flow of raw materials, commodities, and energy, and possess spaces that act as both means of production and forces of production. In fact, we might say that cities are gigantic exchange value entities wherein the process of urbanization is inextricably wedded to the "general law of capitalist accumulation." For a few pages in *Capital*, Marx himself hints at such a dynamic articulation: "'Improvements of towns, which accompany the increase of wealth, such as the demolition of badly built districts, the erection of palaces to house banks, warehouses, etc., the widening of streets for business traffic, for luxury carriages, for the introduction of tramways, obviously drive the poor away into even worse and more crowded corners. . . . The antagonistic character of capitalist accumulation, and thus of capitalist property relations in general, is here so evident. . . . This evil makes such progress alongside the development of industry, the accumulation of capital and the growth and 'improvement' of towns."[1]

And yet, at the same time, cities are also places where people live, establish communities, raise kids, and put down roots. Cities are made up of neighborhoods in which people yearn for comfort, find security, and, occasionally, get angry and organize. To that extent, cities possess distinctive use-value characteristics; sometimes these can be used as launch pads for urban politics, for a politics that battles for what the French urbanist, Henri Lefebvre, once called the "right to the city"—the right to participate in urbanity, the right to appropriate the city not merely as an economic unit, but as a home and as an expression of lived experience.[2] It is this collision of mutual exigencies of urban space, as well as the exigencies of competing factions of society within this space, that prompt conflicts *in* and *over* the city. These conflicts boil down to use versus exchange value dramas, even though they are frequently mediated by various state institutions and crosscut by intervening social and cultural circumstances. In other words, these conflicts have their own specificity while they internalize structural generality. Here Lefebvre is surely right when he says that "although urban space is not analyzed in *Capital*, certain concepts, such as exchange value and use value, today apply to space."[3]

In this concluding chapter, I want to examine the specifically urban meaning of the use value and exchange value contradiction. This dialectical contradiction needs to be seen not in abstract terms but as immanent to the actual texture of urban life. To explicate this claim, I will draw on four intertwining themes central to Marx's thought: fetishism, class, practice, and species-being. Of these four aspects, fetishism and class are culled from *Capital*—in other words, from his mature oeuvre. Species-being comes from the youthful, humanist Marx, from a precocious twenty-six-year-old endeavoring to jettison his Hegelian legacy. Practice is prominent in the works of the mature and young man alike. If anything, practice—or praxis—is the undercurrent

in Marx's whole intellectual development, and endures as the central
tenet of Marxism itself. In what follows, I will attempt to give each a
richer urban content and use it to tie together the loose ends of the
foregoing narrative. Marx's ideas can help flag the preconditions of a
negative dialectic of the city, of a city where urban dwellers look the
negative in the face, not only living with it, but making this negative a
positive force: a power for action and change that doesn't depend on
any preordained movement of history or utopian fantasy.

THE FETISHISM OF URBANIZATION

A recent study conducted by the National Low-Income Housing Coalition indicates that there's no city in the entire United States where a
family living on minimum wage could afford a decent apartment.[4] In
seventy metropolitan regions, minimum wage earners would need to
work for more than 100 hours a week to pay any market rent. High
rents, in turn, prevent average families from saving enough for a home
down payment. That the production of housing is overwhelmingly
geared toward high-end accommodation, toward producing what
Lefebvre calls "abstract spaces," is pretty evident from the dearth of
affordable housing around today. In 1970, there were 6.5 million low-
cost units and slightly over 6 million renter households. Now, there are
6.1 million low-income units and 10.5 million renter households, a
staggering mismatch.

Between 1981 and 1999, when New York City's population expanded
350,000, it added only 42,000 new affordable rental units in response.
Since 1975, median rents in New York increased 33 percent while median incomes grew 3 percent.[5] Wages for middle-level and low-end jobs
actually fell during the 1990s by 7.6 percent and 9.5 percent respectively, after adjusting for inflation.[6] In the city's five boroughs, moreover,
meeting bare-bones needs costs two to five times more than the officially designated poverty threshold of $14,150 per year for a household of
three. In Queens, an adult with a preschool and a school-age child
would need at least $46,836 to get by; in Manhattan, that same family
would need $74,232.[7]

Thus, despite record budget surpluses and eight years of unprecedented national economic expansion and prosperity—destined to be given
away to the already wealthy via George W. Bush's tax-cut bonanza—there

is little public concern about the poor or about affordable housing. In most cities, people seem to have to scramble to make ends meet, taking several jobs to cope with the perpetual rises in housing costs—even a shabby single room or a windowless garage now cost the earth. Indeed, near San Jose, in Silicon Valley, where many high-tech and high-flying Nasdaq-listed companies have their HQs, the Mexican janitors who clean them are compelled to live with their families in windowless garages. This is what $7 an hour gets you in a booming region, replete with its dot-com millionaires and high-tech professionals—even a garage costs $750 per month, well over half a monthly paycheck. The garages are rented out illegally, of course. These wealthy "post-industrial" corporations, who symbolize and drive the "New Economy," invariably wash their hands of poverty wages and the living conditions of their menial employees, saying janitors aren't their employees, but rather those of the cleaning contractor. "In Mexico," said one woman janitor, Alicia, working at Sun Microsystems, "people tell you all these great stories about the United States, that there is money on the ground that you can grab with your own hands. People never tell you how hard it is to make it here."[8] In the end, the process of urbanization produces a rather bleak experience of urbanism for a lot of city folks, for America's urban working class, whose ranks are vividly growing not shrinking. With an imaginative reworking, Marx can help us puncture this paradox, can expose this "fetishism," can help us figure out how prosperity *produces* deepening poverty, and how it has its own contradictory spatial logic.

"Fetishism of commodities" is one of Marx's profoundest ideas. The discussion, appearing at the end of the first chapter of *Capital*, tells us plenty about the "commodity form" under capitalism. But it has tremendous purchase on life and knowledge in general, and we can deepen and extend its key message. It emphasizes something very important about how the world appears to us. It urges us to remember that while appearances are real, they're also absentminded. Once we address this amnesia, Marx believes the way we see and understand our world, and our place in it, will dramatically alter. Indeed, this perspective shift will be grist for our political mill, one that gives us a firmer grip on how society functions and what we must do to change it.

Central to the idea is the apparent paradox that commodities are "sensuous that are at the same time supra-sensible or social."[9] These products of labor aren't false, Marx says, since they do have actual materiality, they are created by human beings through specific forms of work. There's nothing phony about this appearance; but this is merely one part of the story. There's another tale to tell, insists Marx, because a commodity's physicality, its palpable "thing" quality, bears little or no connection to the social relations that made it. As an "it" we hear nothing about productive relationships between workers and owners, between minimum wage toilers and rich bosses, between factory hands and corporate CEOs, between Nike sole makers in Vietnam and stockbrokers on Wall Street, between janitors cleaning Silicon Valley offices and winking Nasdaq shares in Times Square. Intersubjective human relations, relations emerging through a particular social organization and mode of production, are henceforth perceived by people as objective. Its thing-like aura disguises a commodity's social content, occludes its process basis. Form belies content; we can perceive a thing, but a process and a social relation is somehow beyond our grasp, somehow imperceptible and untouchable, invisible, and odorless. The masking effect, the blurring of content by "mist-enveloped" form, essence by "mystical" appearance, Marx deems fetishism. "It is precisely this finished form of the world of commodities—the money form," Marx says, "which conceals the social character of private labor and the social relations between individual workers, by making those relations appear as relations between material objects, instead of revealing them plainly."[10]

The upshot, for Marx, is that the world of capitalism is at once a thing and a process, having an observable outcome as well as an unobservable "law of motion." As far as he's concerned, we must conceptualize the *experience* and *production* of the world not as either/or, but as *both simultaneously*. Marx conceived reality radically at odds with the Cartesian partitioning of subject from object, cause from effect, mind from matter. In a nutshell, Marx demands that we grasp perceptible experience and imperceptible processes as one *concrete totality*.

This was also the aim of Henri Lefebvre, who put a distinctive urban and spatial spin on fetishism. He urges us not to fetishize space, not to view it as merely a thing, not to see buildings, monuments, public spaces, entire neighborhoods, and urban infrastructure as just "objects in space." Instead, we had to make a conceptual leap. The "production of space" can thus be likened to the production of actual "thing" commodities. Space in cities is colonized and commodified, created and torn down, bought and sold, used and abused, speculated on and fought over. Space is highly contested terrain, to be sure, and invariably the highest or most powerful bidder wins. We can usually see their spoils inscribed in the city's built form, often towering above us or else walling us off. Now, Lefebvre warned, Marxist urban theory has to trace out the dynamic and complex interplay of the space-commodity much the same way as Marxist economic theory traces out the dynamic and complex interplay of thing-commodities. Now, urban theory must delve into space's fluid movement, into its generative moments, into its actual production, hooking up this process with the outcome of the process.[11] From this standpoint, we can then open out the canvas, likewise envision the city itself as a specific observable experience as well as a supra-sensible productive process. From this standpoint, these realms represent two epistemological moments within an ontological unity; one we experience—*urbanism*—the other we don't—*urbanization*—but know it really exists nonetheless.

Urbanism, we might say, is specific, urbanization general; urbanism is concrete and about use values, urbanization abstract and about exchange values. Maybe urbanism resembles Marx's "concrete labor" while urbanization has greater affinity with "abstract labor." Maybe we should push Marx a bit further, insofar as "abstract" for him tended to operate within a purely temporal orbit. He held that qualitatively different (concrete) labor activities under capitalism get reduced to a single quantitative yardstick: money, the universal measure of value. This standard becomes the common denominator of all things as commodity relations colonize everywhere and everybody. Marx coined this kind of labor *abstract labor*, labor in general, labor intimately tied to the law of value, to socially necessary *labor time*. Needless to say, "abstract" here in no way implies a mental construct: it has a real material existence, just as value does, just as interest rates and stock prices do, despite the fact that nobody can touch, feel, or hear them. Nor is it meant to imply that urbanization isn't specific, either, isn't a process that gets actualized in different ways in different contexts. Rather, the argument is meant to critically frame the totality of the capitalist urban process as a two-fold movement, like the commodity itself; Marx gives us the vocabulary and the mind-set to spot duality in unity, process in form, the abstract in the concrete, generality in particularity. So, in like vein, urbanization conjures up a sort of *abstract space*. It is a process that gains meaningful "objective" expression somewhere, in *concrete space*, in qualitatively different buildings, activities, locales, and modes of social intercourse in and through space, but its underlying concern isn't with distinctive experience. Its being is underwritten by value logistics, which condition the structural coherence of this abstract space, direct the expansive flow and trajectory of urbanization. Therein, banks, real estate interests, corporations, information networks, law and order, are writ large and reign supreme—or try to.

Marx's concept of fetishism equips critical urbanists with the conceptual tools to better understand, criticize, and ultimately challenge the way the built environment of cities is suffused with value and surplus value. It can help unveil "mist-enveloped" forms of urbanization and deepen our knowledge of how, using Harvey Molotch's apt phrase, cities have become huge "growth machines," large-scale agglomerations of fixed capital that lubricate circulating capital and enhance the accumulation of capital.[12] Here cities are compelled to compete with other cities to attract investment, wrestling with each other for relative advantage, trying to lure high-income earners or spenders, command and control functions, cutting-edge corporations and high-tech firms, imploring them all to settle (or stay) in their city, promising goodies in return. In fact, city governments have done almost anything to put their city on the map, anything that improves their place image, quality of life and business climate, anything that makes the city appear tougher and more entrepreneurial. Of course, this scenario has been ongoing for a while now, at least since 1976, when Molotch first aired his seminal thesis. But over the last fifteen years or so, growth and entrepreneurial exigencies have become especially frantic, often life or death struggles for a lot of U.S. cities.

As the Dow has gotten fat and bullish, not only has American industry gotten lean but cities have gotten lean as well, and a sort of "lean urbanization" pervades and dramatizes the current American urban condition, dramatizes people's contemporary experience of urbanism. Just as Wall Street has rewarded corporate shakedowns, job elimination, "downsizing" and "rightsizing," it rewards lean cities, too—or at least rewards landed property and investors within lean cities, those personifications of abstract space, those who can really make space pay. Lean urbanization is the imperceptible process behind neoliberal urban policy; and its progeny, the lean city, is a city that has been actively downsized, one now assuming the status of a business enterprise, typically measuring itself more by the ability to operate efficiently at minimal cost. Cost savings made from living labor (variable capital) are thereby realized in fixed form, in concrete space, veiling its "abstract" basis. The fetishism attaches itself to the urban process as soon as the intimate connection between living labor and the dead labor embodied in these "things in space" is severed, is somehow beyond our capacity to imagine, is reified as a supra-sensible, nonperceptual reality.

The hypertrophy of Wall Street and finance capital has had a profound impact on the U.S. economy and American labor, as well as on the form and function of American cities. Jobs can be sacrificed—indeed, job loss is tolerated—so long as inflation is squeezed. The current fixation on inflation, of course, makes perfect sense from the standpoint of vested powers that be. After all, inflation erodes the value of financial assets, including space as a financial asset, thus undermining ruling class and rentier privilege. The deflationary bias of the Federal Reserve is wittingly pro-business, wittingly pro-FIRE, and the "ruse of inflation" and monetarist quackery ensures its preeminence as the executive committee for managing the common affairs of the bourgeoisie. Now, we're told, rising capital and property values is healthy, but rising labor wages are somehow inflationary. This fuzzy logic justifies keeping real interest rates at a permanently high level, regularly mobilizing hikes as an instrument of class war, pitting profits and rents against wages.

Real estate values and rents have risen exponentially over the 1990s at the same time as labor values and wage levels have either stagnated or fallen in actual spending power terms. Between 1979 and 1997, average hourly wages for white-collar clerical staff fell from $14.58 to $12.82, after adjusting for inflation; over the same period, median hourly incomes for male nonsupervisory employees fell $2.20, hurting younger workers most.[13] The $5.15 federal minimum wage is really worth a good deal less than it was in 1968; working people are generally putting in longer hours, experience greater job insecurity, and usually have less health coverage. Contingent work lay at the heart of the Clinton boom and was the central lever of U.S. capitalist accumulation during the 1990s.[14] Its net urban result, as it unfolds over and through space, is that housing costs now invariably outpace salaries, dead labor de-couples itself from living labor.

THE MAKING OF THE WORKING CLASS
IN THE CITY

In a sense, what it means to be working class now gets defined by the twofold character of urbanism, by the collision of lean urbanization with the reality and experience of people's lives. Class, in other words, is how the process and the experience really get actualized, how one impedes and invades the other, on the ground, somewhere and at sometime. Class in the city, we might say, is now forged by the dialectic of urbanization and urbanism. It's precisely this clash, this dialectic, which is *making* the urban working class in the United States and elsewhere. And its members are present at their own making. The participation of the working class in their own formation is brilliantly described in Edward Thompson's *Making of the English Working Class*: "Class happens when some men, as a result of common experiences (inherited or shared), feel and articulate the identity of their interests as between themselves, and as against other men whose interests are different from (and usually opposed to) theirs." Thompson reminds us how Marx defined class not as a "thing," but as a fluid relationship that "evades analysis if we attempt to stop it dead at any given moment and anatomize its structure."

Although it's true that Marx left a fair bit of unfinished business on the class front, it's nonetheless evident that he posited neither a sociological definition of class nor any theory of social stratification. While his only direct confrontation with class petered out after a page and a half at the end of *Capital,* volume 3, we know he never saw class as an occupational category or as a rigid, quantifiable numbers game assessed by the census. Instead, he theorized class as a dynamic process, as an intricate battle of roles and relationships, in which individuals become "bearers" of economic categories and interests, interests that are changeable over time and space. For Marx, the role played by the group he labeled the "modern working class" was—and still is—necessarily complex. Sometimes, for instance, the role and interests of its members is ambiguous; sometimes their constitution changes, their "personification" of labor power has them wear many hats, dress in different clothes, live in pretty suburban houses as well as downtown single rooms. As an experiential being, the working class uses its brains, hands, and feet to make something useful or to provide a service for somebody else in exchange for a wage. Other times, the working class's enslavement to capital is "concealed by the variety of individual capitalists to whom it sells itself."[15]

None of this, though, annuls the fact that its members must labor in some way to earn a living. Nothing here annuls the fact that ostensibly disparate people—in their dirty overalls or pressed suits, sweating in factories or Web searching in offices, researching in labs or teaching in universities—constitute a class of laborers "who live only so long as they find work, and who find work only so long as their labor increases capital." They constitute the modern working class, whether they know it or not. Neither does the "unproductive" service nature of much twenty-first-century work undermine Marx's class prognosis. Quite the reverse: it actually offers definitive proof of his class theory. Three-quarters of the way through *Capital*'s pivotal chapter on "Machinery and Large-Scale Industry," Marx demonstrated how the technological development of the productive forces necessitates a service sector class. So what looks like the disappearance of the "traditional" (blue-collar) working class is, for him, but a reconstitution of this class. The burgeoning of a service class thereby reflects a deepening of capital-labor relations not its supersession. For, he concludes, "the extraordinary increase in the productivity of large-scale industry, accompanied as it is by both a more intensive and a more extensive exploitation of labor-power in all spheres of production, permits a larger and larger part of the working class to be employed unproductively."[16]

Marx is referring here to the unproductive labor of the "servant classes," "domestic slaves," "lackeys," constantly expanding in numbers, who toil for the rich. It doesn't take too much imagination to update these occupational groupings, and in our day see this servant class in its home care guise, or as retail store and restaurant workers, hamburger flippers, janitors, security guards, and the like. Even when Marx wrote *Capital,* the largest part of the working class wasn't the blue-collar factory variety—stereotypically recognized as his agents of revolutionary transformation—but an "unproductive" servant class. Marx knew this. In England and Wales in the 1860s, he says, those employed in textile factories, mines, and metal industries, taken together, were still less than the number of domestic modern slaves.

"What an elevating consequence of the capitalist exploitation of machinery!"[17] Simply put, technological expansion under capitalism *actively produces* an unproductive service class. As the mode of production develops, what looks like the disappearance of the "traditional" working class is, in actuality, a reconstitution of this traditional working class. The growth of a service class reflects a *deepening* of capital-labor relations, not its supersession. That we are said to be living in a high-tech "postindustrial" society is definitive proof of Marx's class theory, not reason to abandon it.

Both productive and unproductive workers have steadily come to recognize their common interests—common working-class interests—and have begun to behave with *class consciousness*. They've begun, in short, to put class into practice. Class consciousness and class practice emerge when the fetishism between process and experience is punctured, when the unintelligible process is rendered intelligible in daily life, when a common, shared experience is identified and comprehended. When those who once identified with the big guys suddenly discovered downsizing, they soon began to identify with the little guys; when those once working with their brains felt the brunt of de-skilling, they began to bond with those laboring with their hands; when those pushing paper by day had their benefits cut, they found common ground with those cleaning offices by night. That is class consciousness. It is when people realize that what privileges they may have had were really contingent all along.[18] It's when single-room occupants resist landlord harassment, when people demand their rights to shelter, collectively resist gentrification, appeal for a living wage. All these people, in one way or another, have been exposed to the vicissitudes of competition, to the vagaries of supply and demand for their labor power, to market fluctuations in real estate, to the wrath of exchange value. Now these people know they're dispensable, know they're relative to the ebb and flow of capital accumulation. Knowing this is what Marx meant by class consciousness. It's a sobering experience, to be sure, yet it's a political experience, too.

"PRACTICING" CLASS IN THE CITY

Collective awareness and shared experience—class consciousness—is the impetus behind the organizing drives and collective forms of struggle now scattered throughout urban America. People are uniting in their communities and workplaces, and they're pinpointing the necessity of guarding both flanks at once. Living wage campaigns, for instance, seek to unite people in efforts to establish standards for the contracting-out of public services; in applying conditions on tax abatements and public subsidy; in demanding "claw-back" provisions if corporations downsize or fail to deliver on stipulated promises; and in seeking outright increases in the minimum wage. Now a living wage constitutes a "family wage," a "housing wage," remuneration that enables workers and their dependents to live with dignity in the city, to play a little as well as work hard, to reproduce as they produce. Activists' demands here chime with those Marx set out at the beginning of the "Working Day" chapter of *Capital*: "You are constantly preaching to me the gospel of 'saving' and 'abstinence,'" Marx has one worker say to a boss. "Very well! Like a sensible, thrifty owner of property I will husband my sole wealth, my labor-power, and abstain from wasting it foolishly. Every day I will spend, set in motion, transfer into labor only as much of it as is compatible with its normal duration and healthy development. . . . What you gain in labor, I lose in substance of labor. Using my labor and despoiling it are quite different things."[19]

The notion of a *living* wage, with its biological and corporeal overtones, has a universality that is bringing together different kinds of people, with different skin colors and ethnicities and gender, in different kinds of work, in many different kinds of cities, to bond in novel and unexpected ways. Here, people have started to wise up; they're increasingly recognizing how subsidized waterfront redevelopment and the contracting-out of city service work are not only inexorably linked, they've spawned poverty-wage jobs as well. Those ubiquitous downtown convention centers, hotels, neighborhood upscaling, new sports stadiums, have guzzled gallons of public alms, yet soup kitchen lines in a lot of cities lengthen, missions still find steady work most nights, and affordable housing is a bygone memory. Social struggles of these sorts—like those that we have seen Baltimore, Liverpool, Los Angeles, and New York—have launched offensive, confrontational politics, often bypassing the effete ballot box system. They've crystallized Marx's insistence in *Capital* that political struggles are invariably sanctioned by force, resolved by the respective power of the combatants. "The question whether objective truth can be attributed to human thinking," Marx said back in 1845, "is not a question of theory but is a *practical* question. Humans must prove the truth, i.e. the reality and power, the this-sidedness of their thinking in practice. The dispute over the reality or non-reality of thinking that is isolated from practice is a purely *scholastic* question."[20]

It is through practical struggle, through practical engagement, that truth is both discovered and created; it's through practical collective struggle, Marx says, that people can find and remake themselves, change the world while changing their own nature. Marx knows that practice is vitally important for defining what it means to be human, for taking us beyond "one-sided," purely contemplative, isolated beings. To be sensuous, to feel yourself and other people around and alongside you, necessitates practical activity. Social struggles, for Marx, are at the same time existential voyages. Sometimes these struggles erupt out on to the city street itself, into urban public space. Here, grievances about the wage relation and about the housing relation—grievances about the whole *urban question,* if we may extend Frederick Engels's old manifesto—is about creating an institutional culture and civic space that enables practice to unfurl.

Maybe what cities need, more than anything else, are spaces and institutions where this practice develops in a context of free association. Freely associative practice can, in turn, help light and air seep into city and working life. Lean urbanization has darkened and asphyxiated a lot of American cities, has created predictable ubiquity, homogeneous urban landscapes in which financially successful initiatives are serially reproduced. And if there are any public spaces here, they're usually sterile and stupefying, air-conditioned nightmares that desensitize experience rather than intensify it. And within their interstices, assorted service workers toil for long hours, receive pittances in return, and travel great distances for this pittance. And when they get home, they pinch pennies for the rent. Rarely do we find ethical and aesthetical urban spaces coexisting. In fact, rarely do we find Marx's mature ethical invocations about revolutionary practice and his youthful existential evocations about freedom and passions ever coexisting. The former vision is workerist and Promethean; the latter, playful and Orphean. We need to invent urban practices and spaces that can conjoin both, that promote a dialogue between the two stances as well as a confrontation between the two currents in

Marx. Meanwhile, there's plenty to be done to make the interim feel less transitory, plenty that's already being done to make it feel more lived in, more passionate.

STRUGGLE AND SPECIES-BEING: URBANISM AND HUMAN DISSATISFACTION

When he was honeymooning in Paris in 1844, Marx wrote how "the practical creation of an *objective world*, the *fashioning* of inorganic nature, is proof that man is a conscious species-being."[21] Marx puts a lot of emphasis on the way we practically and consciously make our world, the way we make it "actively and actually," the way we wrestle with the reality outside of our own thinking minds. We do this wrestling together, Marx assures us, and thus we collectively produce ourselves and our kind; we produce, in his words, our own "species-life," quite literally making how we think and act, feel and see. For Marx, problems of our world—real social dilemmas—are approachable and resolvable only in a practical way, "only through the practical energy of man." The "reality of our essential powers" is especially tangible in our "species-activity," in our own "everyday, material industry." The way we labor, the way we struggle every day, shaping our lives, consciously and thoughtfully, makes us unique and distinguishes us from other animals. We are special because we are equipped with what Marx called "*vital powers*." These powers exist in all of us as "dispositions," "capacities," and "*drives*." These drives energize us as human beings, define our nature, spur us on somehow. At the same time, the "objects" of these drives are objects that exist outside us, exist independently of us, and yet are "indispensable to the exercise and confirmation of our essential powers." We've got to have them, and as we try to get them we become sensuous.

Marx thought that a being without any object outside itself is no being at all, is somebody who exists merely in themselves, not *for themselves*, lives in a state of solitude. "As soon as I have an object," he claims, "this object has me for its object. But a non-objective being is an unreal, non-sensuous, merely thought, i.e. merely conceived being, a being of abstraction." "To be sensuous," Marx insists, "i.e. to be real, is to be an object of sense, a *sensuous* object, and thus to have sensuous objects outside one's sense perception." It is our driving and wrestling to connect with this sensuous external world—a sensuous world that incorporates other people—reaching out, feeling and seeing and yearning, not turning inward and contemplating, that ensures we're *passionate* beings. And passion, Marx holds, "is man's essential power vigorously striving to attain its object."[22] While his language is abstract and vague, even a little woolly, Marx is nonetheless trying to affirm the struggle for "free-conscious activity" in the "species-character" of men and women. Objective reality—the external objects and world that surround us, that contextualizes our existence—can condition this free-conscious activity and struggle; it can constrain it, obviously; but it can also enable it, nourish any struggle and human yearning, inspire our essential powers.

The young Marx gave a central place to the ideal of a society and environment in which the possibilities for passion, striving, dreaming, and acting practically could heighten. He championed a social and psychological space in which the possibilities for adventure and intrigue could intensify, where our senses—seeing, feeling, hearing, smelling, tasting, wanting, acting, and loving (all Marx's words)—could blossom as "organs of individuality" and "theoreticians in their immediate praxis." It spells a city, perhaps, where there's intense human experience and struggle, where life is lived without rubber gloves, where spaces—real, material, civic, and cultural—exist to promote and give scope to diverse human striving, where people inhabit a wholesome world a bit like a good farmer's market. There, fruit and vegetables are usually misshapen, often they're dirty and battered, but invariably they taste great, even raw—especially raw. Above all, they *taste,* and in our contemporary processed age that's saying a lot. These are the sort of items that are dumped by big chain supermarkets, who stock only the most perfectly formed, mass-grown specimens, those devoid of dirt and flavor. (And, contrary to the ad men, are relatively more expensive than farmer's market produce.) Marx invoked a somewhere that heightens our senses, stimulates them, makes them richer and more aware, open to "real life." That somewhere would likely be dirty and misshapen: what ensures that we feel is precisely that we vigorously strive and struggle—amid the dirt and with fallibility—for our desideratum. To that degree, Marx challenged us to make a freer and more open-ended society for ourselves, to enact a gaping, passionate city that's the "bringer of plurabilities"—if I may borrow James Joyce's wonderful phrase from *Finnegan's Wake.*

Perhaps, in the last instance, there is no authentic transcendence of the dialectic of urbanization and urbanism, no last instance. Perhaps, instead, progressives need to find ways of incorporating struggle, conflict, and contradiction into a passionate and just urban life, secretly acknowledging that the way beyond these contradictions is working through them, not around them. Then we'll realize that there are no ways beyond them. What's left for the Left is for us to find ways both to live with and struggle against some of these contradictions, harnessing our spirit of resistance, using it creatively, continually to push onward and forward. Dostoevsky's Underground Man says that human beings eternally and continually build roads for themselves, leading somewhere, no matter where, and that the main thing isn't where it leads, "but just that it leads." Urban dwellers and critical urbanists need to internalize this spirit. We can't return to the ideal of the Crystal Palace, but perhaps we can wrestle for a negative dialectics of the city, and in that wrestling and struggling—in that negativity—we might actually discover ourselves as people, might actually devise something democratically positive.

Spaces like Times Square, New York's entire SRO housing stock, its Lower East Side, London's King's Cross, Baltimore's southeast waterfront, Liverpool's Toxteth district, and Los Angeles's east side and South Central—to say nothing of intensive zones of human experience everywhere—are kept alive and energized through conflict and struggle. "Real life," as Marx put it, exists in these spaces, often in microcosmic traces, as it does in a lot of other spaces across urban America. The point for progressives, for anybody who cares about the future of people and about the fate of cities, is to organize and try to make these little oases macrocosmic. This is how ordinary people might *socialize* urban space, might transform it into an arena where use values predominate. "The production of socialist space," Henri Lefebvre reminded us a while ago, "means the end of private property and the state's political domination of space, *which implies the passage from domination to appropriation and the primacy of use over exchange.*"[23] Every day, of course, there's plenty to be done. And in the everyday city, conflict defines the culture and nature of a lot of its internal spaces. Conflict means danger, often it means injustice, always it means life and human yearning, human fascination. Sometimes it means death. Paradoxically, this is often the lifeblood of a vibrant urbanism, of a mixed city, of a radical culture. In the preceding text I have argued as much. Didn't Marx himself reveal the enormous creative power of conflict, of *human dissatisfaction*, of history progressing through its darker side, of the power of lepers struggling at the city gate? It's obvious how much art and literature and human kinship has developed out of conflict. And it's that conflict, that intensity of experience, which makes for compelling stories and attracts avid audiences everywhere.

All of which raises a dangerous and tricky question: Bereft of dissatisfaction, what do humans become and how much creative capacity is lost? It's dangerous because this reasoning can be—and often is—usurped by the Right, who relentlessly promote inequality insofar as it forces people (certain people anyway) to struggle and compete against each other. It's tricky as well because leftists now have to proceed carefully through questions of openness and closure in the city, about an urbanism that's fair yet free, that's just but imperfect, a space where invisible contradictions aren't fetishized and where visible conflicts are confronted without repression. We may never get that far, of course, may never know *how far* we can get in advance. (We may never be quite sure who this "we" is either.) Thus, progressives may never solve the "urban question" the way Engels wanted us to solve the "housing question"—wholesale, in one fell swoop, accepting nothing less. Still, what's crucial here is to express our dissatisfaction collectively, to channel it rationally, to direct it against a common enemy, to utilize it creatively and relentlessly, forever pushing forth with it.

The job, we on the Left already know, is immeasurably aided and enhanced by organizers and activists, whose services and talents are in abundant supply. (We can always use a few more dedicated hands, needless to say.) We have plenty of labor and community organizers, assorted organic intellectuals, committed citizens, working-class heroes, living-wagers and progressives of numerous stripes, people who can critically analyze a given situation, can see it as the internalization of previous situations, and can help develop a class practice to contest that situation. These people all know how urban spaces can become bastions of defense and attack, fortresses from which ordinary citizens strategize and energize, recognize some condition and problem; and by trying to solve it, people then recognize that their own particular grievance somewhere coexists with other particular grievances elsewhere, and that those particulars need each other if they are to grow strong. People learn how to generalize as they particularize. They "bond" in one place with people in another place, as the late British socialist Raymond Williams liked to say.[24] That's how a social movement takes shape—how could it otherwise? By bonding, by wedding critical thought to practical struggle and action, everyday people—people like you and me—can construct real cities from below, not inherit phony utopias from above. We can inhabit cities made livable by people struggling to live. Along the way, we might even see a little light in the here and now, a little ray of hope, and discover a kindred community of fellow travelers. As progressives struggle together, as we collectively reach for the stars, we might, at long last, be able to stand upright. And as we do so, we might also see those stars glow in the neon-lit city of night.

Notes

1

1   F. Scott Fitzgerald, "My Lost City," in *The Crack-Up and Other Pieces and Stories* (Harmondsworth: Penguin, 1965). Bunny, of course, was none other than the esteemed critic and adopted New Yorker Edmund Wilson.

2   Ibid., 20–21, 28.

3   Georg Simmel, "The Metropolis and Mental Life," in *On Individuality and Social Forms*, ed. Donald Levine (Chicago: University of Chicago Press, 1971).

4   Fitzgerald, "My Lost City," 28–29.

5   Ibid., 30.

6   See "And City Shall Speak Unto City," *Independent on Sunday*, April 12, 1998.

7   Jane Jacobs, *Cities and the Wealth of Nations* (New York: Random House, 1984), 32.

8   Karl Marx, *Capital*, vol. 1 (Harmondsworth, U.K.: Penguin, 1976), 812.

9   Raymond Williams, *Resources of Hope* (London: Verso, 1982), 243. Original emphasis.

10 Cf. Marshall Berman, "L.A. Raw," *The Nation*, April 1, 1991.

2

1   Neil Smith, "New City, New Frontier: The Lower East Side as Wild, Wild West," in Sorkin (ed) *Variations on a Theme Park: The New American City and the End of Public Space*, ed. M. Sorkin (New York: Noonday Press, 1992), 65.

2   Richard Hurd, *Principles of City Land Values* (New York: The Record & Guide, 1924), 16.

3   See E. Garland, "The End of Baltimore as a Blue-Collar Town," *Baltimore Magazine*, December 1980.

4   Carl Bode, *Mencken* (Baltimore: Johns Hopkins University Press, 1986), 29–30.

5   Jack Kerouac, *The Town and the City* (New York: Harcourt Brace & Co., 1978), 90.

6   Mark Levine, "Downtown Redevelopment as an Urban Growth Strategy: A Critical Appraisal of Baltimore's Renaissance," *Journal of Urban Affairs* 9 (1987):103–23.

7   Garland, "End of Baltimore as a Blue-Collar Town."

8   Peter Szanton, *Baltimore 2000* (Baltimore: Goldseker Foundation), 1986.

9   See "The Yuppies Move Downtown," *Baltimore Magazine*, August 1986.

10 Ibid.

11 City of Baltimore, *Report: East Baltimore Real Estate*, Baltimore, no date.

12 Author's interview with Marion Pines, former commissioner of Baltimore's Neighborhood Progress Administration (NPA), December 4, 1990. NPA is a public agency that "oversees housing, economic development, employment, and housing programs for Baltimore's neighborhoods, as well as for its downtown and Inner Harbor areas."

13 Donald Trump, *The Art of the Deal* (New York: Arrow Books, 1987), 38.

14 Matthew Crenson, *Neighborhood Politics* (Cambridge: Harvard University Press, 1983), 47.

15 Norman Rukert, *Historic Canton* (Baltimore: Bodine & Associates, 1978).

16 Ibid., 20.

17 Sherry Olson, *Baltimore: the Building of an American City* (Cambridge: Ballinger, 1980).

18 Linda Shopes, "Fells Point: Community and Conflict in a Working-Class Neighborhood," Elizabeth Fee, Linda Shopes & Linda Zeidman, ed. *The Baltimore Book: New Views on Local History* (Philadelphia: Temple University Press, 1992).

19 William Stolk, *American Can Company: Revolution in Containers* (New York: Newcombe Publications, 1960).

20 Harry Magdoff and Paul Sweezy, *Stagnation and the Financial Explosion* (New York: Monthly Review Press, 1987).

21 Connie Bruck, *The Predator's Ball: The Inside Story of Drexel, Burnham and the Rise of the Junk Bond Raiders* (New York: Penguin, 1989), 12.

22 The Milken Empire came crashing down in late 1990 when the mighty financier was sentenced to ten years in prison and fined $600 million for securities violations. Still, the Milken legacy will be harder to expunge than the man himself. The "Drexel-Milken saga could be an opportunity to explore this system's shortcomings, but," said a *Nation* editorial (December 17, 1990), "it's being treated mainly as an episode of personal villainy. It isn't, and the pathologies are still with us." The Enron saga is the latest incarnation of these pathologies.

23 Bruck, *The Predator's Ball*, 11.

24 "The New Aces of Low-Tech," *Business Week*, September 15, 1986.

25 Cited in "A 180-Degree Turnabout for Triangle," *Business Week*, December 5, 1988.

26 Ibid.

27 "The Return of Second-Hand Rose," *Fortune*, October 24, 1988.

28 Ibid.

29 "A 180-Degree Turnabout for Triangle," *Business Week*, December 5, 1988

30 "The Rape of the Bondholder," *Forbes*, January 23, 1989.

31 DeCarlo, Richard J., senior vice president Manufacturing and Beverage, American National Can Company, Information Release, August 5, 1987.

31 This information was obtained by Southeast Community Organization (SECO) under the Freedom of Information Act.

32 "The Rape of the Bondholder," *Forbes*, January 23, 1989.

33 Mark Levine, "Downtown Redevelopment as an Urban Growth Strategy," *Journal of Urban Affairs*, 112.

34 These details were made available to me by SECO who obtained the UDAG and financial information under the Freedom of Information Act.

35 "New Canton Rises on Painful Memories," *Baltimore Sun*, June 19, 1988.

36 For instance, those developers most active along the Canton waterfront—like John Paterakis, Louis Grasmick, and Robert Agus—are businessmen who have had close ties with former mayor William Donald Shaefer's political machine.

37 See "In Answer to Neighborhood Concerns, Designer of American Can Site Submit New Plans for Shopping Center with No High Rises," *East Baltimore Guide*, March 31, 1988.

38 Letter to Baltimore's Neighborhood Progress Administration (NPA), May 1988.

39 See "Schmoke Seeks Fells Point, Canton Shoreline Plan," *Baltimore Sun*, February 23, 1988.

40 "Consultant's Scenarios for Waterfront Draw Fire from Developers, Residents," *Baltimore Sun*, July 31, 1988.

41 Cited in "Vandalism and Toxic Spills Blamed By Developer," *East Baltimore Guide*, September 14, 1989.

42 "Banks Strain with Low Growth," *Baltimore Sun*, September 24, 1990.

43 David Harvey, "Flexible Accumulation Through Urbanization: Reflections on 'Postmodernism'" in the American City," *Antipode* 18 (1987): 260–86. Quotation on 281.

44 See "East Baltimore Group Urges Fees on Waterfront Growth," *Baltimore Sun*, September 15, 1989.

45 Dennis Keating, "Linking Downtown Development to Broader Community Goals," *Journal of American Planning Association* 52: 133–41.

46 Cited in "Planners Reject Impact Fees," *Baltimore Sun*, November 2, 1990.

47 Even if any linkage policy does get implemented, wily developers like
Baltimore's Robert Agus would doubtless circumvent such legislation. At a
seminar on "Community Partnerships for Responsible Investment," held at the
University of Maryland on November 15, 1990, Agus suggested you'd probably
see a mushrooming of 49,000-square-foot projects!

3

1   See Michael Parkinson, *Liverpool on the Brink* (Hermitage, U.K.: Policy Journals,
1985), and "Liverpool's Fiscal Crisis: An Anatomy of Failure," in *Regenerating Cities,*
ed. M.Parkinson, B. Foley & D. Judd (Manchester, Eng.: Manchester University
Press, 1988).

2   P. Waller, "The Riots in Toxteth, Liverpool: A Survey," *New Community* 9 (1981–82):
344–53; M. Keith, "'Something Happened': The Problem of Explaining the 1990
and 1981 Riots in British Cities," in *Race and Racism,* ed. P. Jackson (London:
Unwin Hyman, 1987).

3   Cited in A. Gifford et al., *Loosen the Shackles: First Report of the Liverpool 8 Inquiry
into Race Relations in Liverpool* (London: Karia Press, 1989), 51.

4   Liverpool City Planning Department, *Merseyside Development Corporation:
The Liverpool Experience,* Liverpool, 1987.

5   R.Tameen, ed., *Undercurrents: An Illustrated Anthology from the Inner City*
(Liverpool: Strange Publications, 1990).

6   Liverpool Black Caucus, *The Racial Politics of Militant in Liverpool* (London:
Runnymede Trust, 1986), 86, 120. For Militant's spirited defense of their actions
throughout their four-year campaign, see Peter Taafe and Tony Mulhearn,
Liverpool: A City That Dared to Fight (London: Fortress Books, 1988).

7   Jane Jacobs, *The Death and Life of Great American Cities* (Harmondsworth, Eng.:
Penguin, 1961), 44.

8   Gifford et al., *Loosen the Shackles*, 254.

9   See "Crack and the Cropper," *The Guardian*, June 17, 1992.

10 "When the Finger Points on Granby," Merseyside Community Relations
Council newsletter no.12 (1990); cf. Margaret Simey, *Democracy Rediscovered:
A Study of Police Accountability* (London: Pluto Press, 1988).

11 "The Crime Busters from Out of the Sky," *Liverpool Echo*, January 5, 1989.

12 Iris Marion Young, *Justice and the Politics of Difference* (Princeton, N.J.: Princeton
University Press, 1990), 248.

13 Cited in "Granby Triangle Project," *Charles Wootton Newsletter,* no date.

14 "Focus on Liverpool," *Black Housing*, July/September 1994, 29.

15 Rawls, *Political Liberalism* (New York: Columbia University Press, 1993), xvi–xvii.
16 Ibid., 59.
17 Ibid., 61.
18 Susan Fainstein, "Justice, Politics, and the Creation of Urban Space," in *The Urbanization of Injustice,* ed. A. Merrifield and E. Swyngedouw, (New York: New York University Press, 1997).
19 Salman Rushdie, "Outside the Whale," in *Imaginary Homelands* (London: Granta, 1991), 100–101.
20 Marshall Berman, "'Justice/Just Us': Rap and Social Justice in America," in *The Urbanization of Injustice,* ed. Merrifield and Swyngedouw.
21 Michael Walzer, "Multiculturalism and Individualism," *Dissent,* Spring 1994, 180.
22 Rushdie, *Imaginary Homelands,* 12.

4

1 See David Harvey, "From Managerialism to Entrepreneurialism: The Transformation of Urban Governance in Late Capitalism," *Geografiska Annaler* 71B (1989): 3–17.
2 Cf. Bernard Frieden and Lynne Sagalyn, *Downtown, Inc.* (Cambridge, Mass: MIT Press, 1989).
3 Cited in Robert Pollin and Stephanie Luce, *The Living Wage: Building a Fair Economy* (New York: The New Press, 1998), 64.
4 *Cf.* Fredric Jameson, "Postmodernism, or the Cultural Logic of Late Capitalism," *New Left Review,* no. 146 (1984): 53–92.
5 Mike Davis, "Trying to Build a Union Movement in Los Angeles," *Los Angeles Times* (hereafter *LAT*), March 20, 1994.
6 Eric Mann, "Video Age Reaches Union Bargaining," *LAT,* June 26, 1992.
7 Harold Meyerson, "No Justice, No Growth," *L.A. Weekly,* July 17, 1998.
8 Harold Meyerson, "Contracting-out of Poverty: Downtown Hotel Pact Sets New Standard for L.A.'s Service Sector," *L.A. Weekly,* January 23, 1998.
9 Council Approves 'Living Wage' Law for City Contracts," *LAT,* March 19, 1997.
10 "Defiant Mayor Vetoes 'Living Wage' Ordinance," *LAT,* March 28, 1997.
11 "City Council Approves 'Living Wage' Law," *LAT,* March 19, 1997.
12 "A Boss for a New Generation Broadens Big Labor Appeal: An Interview with Miguel Contreras," *LAT,* January 31, 1999.
13 Cited in Roger Waldinger et al., "Justice for Janitors," *Dissent,* Winter 1997, 41.
14 SEIU Local 399 Report, *A Penny for Justice: Janitors and L.A.'s Commercial Real Estate Market,* Los Angeles, March 1995, 10.
15 "Janitors' Union Vows to Turn Up Organizing Heat," *LAT,* March 26, 1997.

16 "Janitors' Union Uses Pressure and Theatrics to Expand Its Ranks,"
    Wall Street Journal, March 21, 1994.

17 Mike Davis, "Magical Realism: Latinos Reinvent the U.S. Big City," *New Left
    Review,* no. 234 (1999), 35; Andy Merrifield, "A Chronicle of a City Foretold," *New
    Left Review,* November/December 2000, 155–60.

18 "Most Century City Janitors Decide to Walk Off the Job," *LAT,* May 31, 1990.

19 "Panel is Critical of Police Acts," *LAT,* November 21, 1990.

20 Cited in David Bacon, "United They Stand—Justice for Janitors Jockeys for
    Power," *L.A. Weekly,* February 28–March 6, 1997; see also "Janitors: New Drive to
    Recruit Service Workers," *LAT,* March 26, 1997.

21 SEIU Local 1877, "Respect at LAX!", *Activist,* Winter 1998–99, Los Angeles, 4.

22 Marc Cooper, "Busting the Union Busting," *The Nation,* March 2, 1998, 16.

23 Kate Bronfenbrenner, et al., "Preparing for the Worst: Organizing and Staying
    Organized in the Public Sector," in *Organizing to Win: New Research on Union Strate-
    gies,* ed. Bronfenbrenner et al. (Ithaca, N.Y.: Cornell University Press, 1998),
    262–82; see also, Andrew Hacker, "Who's Sticking to the Union?," *The New York
    Review of Books,* February 18, 1999.

24 Thomas L. Palley, *Plenty of Nothing: The Downsizing of the American Dream and the Case
    of Structural Keynesianism* (Princeton, N.J.: Princeton University Press, 1998), 130.

25 For further details, see Andy Merrifield, "Class Formation, Capital Accumula-
    tion, and the Downsizing of America," *Monthly Review,* October 1999, 32–43.

26 Cf. Marshall Berman, "Unchained Melodies: Review of the 150th edition of 'The
    Communist Manifesto,'" *The Nation,* May 11, 1998. This idea pretty much tallies
    with David Harvey's fluid definition of class: "positionality in relation to processes
    of capital accumulation." See *Justice, Nature and the Geography of Difference* (Oxford,
    Eng.: Basil Blackwell, 1996), 359.

27 See www.newparty.org/livwag/ and www.livingwagecampaigns.org/.

28 "More Than Money, They Miss the Pride a Good Job Brought," *New York Times,*
    March 5, 1996.

29 Pollin and Luce, *The Living Wage,* 76.

30 See David Harvey, "The Urban Process Under Capitalism: A Framework for
    Analysis," in *The Urban Experience* (Oxford, Eng.: Basil Blackwell, 1989), 74.

31 "Living Wage Ordinance Both Delights and Divides," *New York Times,* May 29, 2001.

32 Pollin and Luce, *The Living Wage,* 81.

33 Waldinger et al., "Justice for Janitors," 42.

34 Kim Moody, *Workers in a Lean World: Unions in the International Economy* (London:
    Verso, 1997), 276.

35 "Boston Enacts Living Wage Rule," *Albany* (N.Y.) *Times-Union,* August 14, 1997.

36 Pollin and Luce, *The Living Wage*, 17 (italics in original). Cf. chapter 4, "How Much Do Living Wage Laws Cost and Who Pays for Them?"

5

1 Dante, *Inferno*, Canto XXVII, 1–3, trans. Robert Pinsky, (New York: Farrar, Strauss & Giroux, 1994).

2 Cf. Marshall Berman, "L.A. Raw," *The Nation*, April 1, 1991.

3 See Ed Soja, *Postmodern Geographies* (London: Verso, 1989); and *Third Space: Journeys to Los Angeles and Other Real-and-Imagined Places* (Oxford, Eng.: Basil Blackwell, 1996); Fredric Jameson, "Postmodernism, or the Cultural Logic of Late Capitalism," *New Left Review* 146: 53–92; Michael Sorkin, "See You in Disneyland," in *Variations on a Theme Park: The New American City and the End of Public Space*, ed. M. Sorkin (New York: Noonday Press, 1992); and *Exquisite Corpse: Writings on Buildings* (London: Verso, 1991). The latter book is a series of vignettes written originally for Sorkin's architecture column in New York's *Village Voice*. Sorkin demonstrates considerable literary flair and chutzpah as he takes to task the official planning, architectural, and real estate profession in his hometown. Nevertheless, Sorkin seduces himself as well as his readers. What would New York be without glamour and dirty dealings and corruption? And why would anybody read Sorkin if they weren't turned on? Elizabeth Wilson makes a similar argument with respect to Jameson's now classic essay—"He [Jameson] himself converts what he loathes into something meaningful in aesthetic terms"—"The Rhetoric of Urban Space," *New Left Review* 209: 146–60.

4 Wilson, "Rhetoric of Urban Space," 160.

5 Carl E. Schorske, "The Idea of the City in European Thought: Voltaire to Spengler," in *Urbanism in World Perspective: A Reader,* ed. Sylvia Fleis Fava (New York: Thomas Crowell Inc., 1968), 409–24.

6 Charles Baudelaire, *Selected Writings on Art and Literature* (Harmondsworth, Eng.: Penguin, 1972) 106–7.

7 Baudelaire, *Les Fleurs Du Mal,* (London: Everyman, 1982).

8 Baudelaire, *Selected Writings on Art and Literature*, 402–03.

9 T. S. Eliot, *To Criticize the Critic and Other Writings* (London: Faber and Faber, 1965), 126. Alas, Eliot couldn't live with the consequences of this lesson. He also felt Baudelaire couldn't go all the way with this thesis either. For example, in his introduction to Baudelaire's *Intimate Journals*, Eliot quotes T. E. Hulme, suggesting, "Baudelaire would have approved: 'A man is essentially bad, he can only accomplish anything of value by discipline—ethical and political. Order is thus not merely negative but creative and liberating. Institutions are necessary.'"

10 Schorske, "Idea of the City," 421.

11 Baudelaire, *Selected Writings on Art and Literature,* 106.

12 See Alexis de Jonge, *Dostoevsky and the Age of Intensity* (London: St. Martin's Press, 1975).

13 Ibid., 37. Still, de Jonge commits a howler when he says that for Dostoevsky and Baudelaire "the city is the root cause of contemporary trauma and spiritual loss" p. 40.

14 Fyodor Dostoevsky, *Crime and Punishment,* trans. Michael Scammell (New York: Washington Square Press, 1968), 64.

15 Fanger, *Dostoevsky and Romantic Realism* (Cambridge: Harvard University Press, 1965).

16 Dostoevsky, *Notes from Underground and The Grand Inquisitor, with relevant works by Chernyshevsky, Shehedrin, and Dostoevsky,* trans. Ralph Matlaw (New York: Meridian, 1991), 6.

17 De Jonge, *Dostoevsky and the Age of Intensity,* 64. It's worth mentioning that Dostoevsky's savage portrayals of human misery and degradation received both sympathetic and unfavorable hearings from the Russian Left. Dobrolyubov, a radical of the 1860s generation, thought Dostoevsky a great humanist writer and compassionate about the humiliated man. Dostoevsky, says Dobrolyubov, concerned himself with "downtrodden people" and searched "their soul for glimmerings of human dignity and protest." On the other hand, Mikhailovski thought Dostoevsky was a "cruel talent" who held a morbid inclination to wallow in the sufferings of the downtrodden, especially in his later works. He suggested Dostoevsky expressed a style of "gratuitous and aimless torture and sadism" that bordered on delighting in human degradation. See also Vladimir Seduro, *Dostoevski in Russian Literary Criticism* (New York: Columbia University Press, 1957), 30–32.

18 Dostoevsky, *Notes from Underground,* 26.

19 Ibid., 42. Emphasis added.

20 Ibid., 31.

21 Rufus Mathewson, *The Positive Hero in Russian Literature* (New York: Columbia University Press, 1958), 19.

22 Chernyshevsky, *What Is To Be Done,* in Dostoevsky, *Notes from Underground,* 167–69.

23 Marshall Berman, *All That Is Solid Melts into Air* (London: Verso, 1983), 235–48.

24 Dostoevsky, *Winter Notes on Summer Impressions* (Evanston, Ill.: Northwestern University Press, 1988), 37.

25 For more details, see Andy Merrifield, "Notes on Suffering and Freedom: An Encounter between Marx and Dostoevsky," *Rethinking Marxism* 11, (1999): 72–86.

26 Karl Marx, "The Economic and Philosophical Manuscripts," in *Marx: Early Writings* (Harmondsworth, Eng.: Penguin, 1974), 389. Citations from this edition are indicated in the text.

27 This, incidentally and interestingly, was the central point of Henri Lefebvre's reinterpretation of the Marx of 1844 in his short book, *Dialectical Materialism*, first published in France in 1939 in response to Joseph Stalin's problematical text, *Historical Materialism*.

28 Jane Jacobs, *Death and Life of Great American Cities* (Harmondsworth, Eng.: Penguin, 1961) 23–25. Citations in text hereafter refer to this article.

29 Lewis Mumford, "The Skyline: Mother Jacobs' Home Remedies," *The New Yorker*, December 1, 1962: 148–79. Citations in text hereafter refer to this article.

30 Donald Miller, *Lewis Mumford: A Life* (New York: Weidenfeld & Nicholson, 1989), 474.

31 Mumford, *The City in History*.

32 Jacobs's concern is developed later in the decade by other notable urbanists like William H. Whyte in *The Last Landscape* (New York: Doubleday, 1968) and Richard Sennett in *The Uses of Disorder* (New York: Vintage Books, 1970).

33 Alfred Kazin, Introduction, in Theodore Dreiser, *Sister Carrie* (Harmondsworth, Eng.: Penguin, 1981), xi.

34 See Eliott Currie "The Scalpel not the Chainsaw: The U.S. Experience with Public Order," *City* 8 (1997): 132–37.

35 See Bruce Shapiro, "Zero Tolerance Gospel," *Index on Censorship* 4 (1997): 17–23. Shapiro points out that civilian complaints about excessive police force in New York have risen 41 percent since Guiliani came to power in November 1993. The shootings of the innocent and unarmed black men Amadou Diallo and Patrick Dorismond by the NYPD likewise emphasizes how this excessive force often bore a racist tag.

36 It ought to be mentioned that London's metropolitan police force claim not to adopt zero tolerance practices elsewhere in central London. The Charing Cross station police, whose beat includes Soho and the West End, now realize that "moving rough sleepers on does not serve to solve the problem in the long term. It just moves them from one area to another, which satisfies the residents' associations if they are moved on, especially in King's Cross where in some cases they've created major disturbances. Zero tolerance is a knee-jerk reaction. It only works for short period of time. The problem will often come back and often in a worse form that when it started." Author's interview with sergeant of Homelessness Unit, London, January 6, 1998.

37 This book extends the earlier work of James Q. Wilson, whose 1982 article in *Atlantic Monthly* set the tone of much of the conservative debate about ordering disorder in the city. Wilson also writes a complimentary foreword to the latest Kelling and Coles monograph.

38 George Kelling and Catherine Coles, *Fixing Broken Windows* (New York: Simon & Schuster, 1996), 8.

39 Ibid., 42.

40 Shapiro, "Zero Tolerance Gospel," 23.

41 Ibid.

42 See Marshall Berman, "Sign of the Times," *Dissent*, Fall 1997, 76–83.

43 Christine Boyer, "Twice-Told Stories: The Double Erasure of Times Square," in *Strangely Familiar*, ed. Iain Borden et al. (London: Routledge 1996), 80.

44 Lawrence Senelick, "Private Parts in Public Places," in *Inventing Times Square*, ed. William R. Taylor (New York: Russell Sage Foundation, 1991), 329–53.

45 Ibid.

46 William Sherman, *Times Square* (New York: Bantam Books, 1980), 4.

47 John Rechy, *City of Night*, (New York: Grove Press, 1963), 26, 34.

48 *Panegyric* (London: Verso, 1989), 63–64.

49 *New York Times*, December 20, 1999.

50 William Solomon, "More Form than Substance: Press Coverage of the WTO Protests in Seattle," *Monthly Review*, May 2000, 14.

51 Guy Debord, *Comments on The Society of the Spectacle* (New York: Verso, 1988), 8.

52 Ibid., 14.

6

1. Author's interview with Mary Osborne, New York City, July 25, 2000.

2. For more historical details, see Gilbert Osofsky's now classic study *Harlem: The Making of a Ghetto* (Chicago: Ivan R. Dee Publishers, 1963).

3. Author's interview with Elizabeth Kane, New York City, August 7, 2000.

4. Author's interview with Terry Poe, New York City, August 17, 2000.

5. See "Housing Crisis Confounds Prosperous City," *New York Times*, July 9, 2000.

6. See "Empty Promises," *City Limits Magazine*, January 2001, 13–14.

7. "SRO Limbo," *The Village Voice*, January 22, 2002.

8. "HUD Plans to Rebuild Houses Caught in Mortgage Scandal," *New York Times*, January 18, 2001.

9. Author's interview with Elizabeth Kane, New York City, August 7, 2000.

10. "11% Visitors Rise Makes City No. 2 U.S. Tourist Destination," *New York Times*, August 8, 2000.

11. "Hotel Occupancy Rate in New York Hit Record Level in 2000," *New York Times*, February 21, 2001.

12. Author's interview with Leah Porter, New York City, August 3, 2000.

7

1   Karl Marx, *Capital*, vol. 1 (New York: Vintage, 1977), 812.

2   Henri Lefebvre, "The Right to the City" in *Henri Lefebvre—Writings on Cities*, ed. and trans. Eleonore Kofman and Elizabeth Lebas (Oxford, Eng.: Blackwell, 1996).

3   Henri Lefebvre, "Space: Social Product and Use Value" in ed. J. Freiberg *Critical Sociology: European Perspectives* (New York: Irvington Publishers, 1979), 292.

4   See Peter Dreier, "Why America's Workers Can't Pay the Rent," *Dissent*, Summer 2000, 38–44.

5   "Housing Crisis Confounds a Prosperous City," *New York Times*, July 9, 2000.

6   At the same time, Giuliani instituted a series of tax incentives in Lower Manhattan to stimulate the rehabilitation of older office buildings. And for those big and rich corporations that threatened to flee pricey Manhattan for the cost-effective New Jersey shoreline, like Credit Suisse First Boston, Merrill Lynch, and Time Warner et al., the mayor offered substantial tax breaks.

7   "In New York, Family Costs Rise Far Above Poverty Line," *New York Times*, September 13, 2000.

8   "Janitors Struggle at the Edge if Silicon Valley's Success," *New York Times*, April 18, 2000. Mike Garcia, President of SEIU Local 1877, reckoned these high-tech firms are hiding behind subcontracting rules to dodge responsibility for their low-rung staff. Something is wildly askew, he said, when Silicon Valley stars like Cisco Systems and Sun Microsystems rake in millions in stock options while those sweeping up their mess earn so little that they live in garages.

9   Marx, *Capital*, vol. 1, 165.

10 Ibid., 168–69.

11 Henri Lefebvre, *The Production of Space* (Oxford, Eng.: Blackwell, 1991).

12 Harvey Molotch, "The City as a Growth Machine: Toward a Political Economy of Place," *American Journal of Sociology* 82, (1976): 309–32

13 Lawrence Mishel, Jared Berstein, and John Schmitt, *The State of Working America, 1998-99* (Ithaca, N.Y.: Cornell University Press, 1999), 131.

14 See Andy Merrifield, "Class Formation, Capital Accumulation, and the Downsizing of America," *Monthly Review*, October 1999, 32–43.

15 Marx, *Capital*, vol. 1, 764.

16 Ibid., 574; see, too, Andy Merrifield, "Marx@2000.com," *Monthly Review*, November 2000, 30–33.

17 Marx, *Capital*, vol. 1, 575.

18 Cf. Marshall Berman, "Unchained Melody," in *Adventures in Marxism*

(New York: Verso, 1999), 263.

19 Marx, *Capital*, vol. 1, 343.

20 "Second Thesis on Feuerbach," in *Marx: Early Writings* (New York: Vintage, 1974), 422. Marx's emphasis.

21 "Economic and Philosophical Manuscripts," in *Marx: Early Writings*, 329. Marx's emphasis.

22 Ibid., 390.

23 Lefebvre, "Space: Social Product and Use Value," 293. Emphasis in original.

24 Raymond Williams, *Resources of Hope* (London: Verso, 1982), 241.

Index